POLICE

this book is for Gene and Brian

The events and images depicted in this publication are not meant to be interpreted or viewed as the visual
counterparts of the text immediately preceding or following a photograph. It is therefore expressly stated that
the images, although depicting actual events that occurred during the preparation of this work in New York City,
do not necessarily coincide with the textual material, nor are they intended to do so.

Copyright © 1983 by Jaydie Putterman
All rights reserved, including the right to reproduce this book or portions thereof in any form.
Published by Holt, Rinehart and Winston, 383 Madison Avenue, New York, New York 10017.
Published simultaneously in Canada by Holt, Rinehart and Winston of Canada, Limited.
Library of Congress Cataloging in Publication Data
Putterman, Jaydie.
Police.
1. New York (N.Y.)—Police—Biography. 2. Gentile,
Gene. 3. McMenamin, Brian. I. Lesur, Rosalynde.
II. Title.
HV8148.N5P87 1982   363.2′092′2 [B]   82-6270   AACR2
ISBN Hardbound: 0-03-062429-0
ISBN Paperback: 0-03-059597-5

First Edition

Printed in the United States of America
1 3 5 7 9 10 8 6 4 2

ISBN 0-03-062429-0 HARDCOVER
ISBN 0-03-059597-8 PAPERBACK

jaydie putterman
rosalynde lesur

POLICE

HOLT, RINEHART AND WINSTON / NEW YORK

I'm a photographer. I take pictures for a living. At one time, *Car and Driver* magazine hired me to photograph the Dodge Monaco. The car was billed as "America's Fastest Sedan," and they called it a Police Pursuit—so it made good sense to photograph it in front of a police station.

One night, I went to the Midtown South Precinct in New York to see about getting permission to take the photographs. And that was the night I met Gene Gentile and Brian McMenamin.

Okay, so when you see a car parked in a "restricted" area in front of the Precinct, what's the first thing you do? Get pissed off, right?

So here's this late-model Dodge with Michigan plates parked dead center in front of the main door. Now maybe this is just some Joe Glomm who's parked there . . . and maybe it's not. Maybe it's an unmarked police car. Anyway, there's only one way to find out. So Gene goes in. And makes a *loud* inquiry as to who is the owner of the car.

Well, the inquiry very quickly points to a hippie-looking guy who's standing there—beard, long hair, everything—talking to a sergeant. And the guy is saying, "Can we take some pictures here?"

"What for?"

"We're doing a magazine article, road-testing this car. We were up in Midtown North, and they wouldn't let us."

So Gene tells him, "Okay, but if you take pictures, 'one hand washes the other.' "

The guy—it turned out his name was Jaydie—asks, "What do you mean?"

"I want to drive the car," Gene says.

"Around the block?"

"No, *not* around the block. I was thinking about the West Side Highway."

Now, at the time, the West Side Highway was closed to all traffic, but there were a couple of stretches in the blocked-off part, maybe a mile or two, where you could just go crazy.

So we jump in our old shebang number 1644, and Jaydie gets in the new Dodge, and we head for the West Side Highway. *Vroom!*

Once we get there, we switch cars. Gene swears he's a natural-born driver—and he sure is.

So now here's Jaydie in the police car, and Gene's driving the Dodge, and it's a drag race on the West Side Highway.

After that, as far as Gene was concerned, Jaydie could drive his car right into the station house and photograph it in front of the desk—provided he'd let Gene drive it too. Which was all right with Jaydie—and by the time he left that night, we'd invited him to sit with us as an observer during our tours.

My wife's name is Rosalynde Lesur; she's from Avignon in the south of France. We both went down to Midtown South some time later; we found Brian and Gene, and then learned that their invitation to be observers wasn't enough—we also needed official permission from "downtown."

"Downtown" is Police Headquarters at 1 Police Plaza, New York City 10013. And the man we were told to speak with was Frank McLoughlin, the deputy commissioner, Public Information. It turned out that we'd have to write a letter explaining what we had in mind. We wrote one describing our purpose as "the photographic documentation of NYPD personnel, particularly in their normal activities and duties."

Armed with this letter, we showed up one morning for an appointment with the deputy commissioner. And a sergeant told us that the deputy commissioner was busy and that it would be better if we came back another day.

"Well, maybe it would be better still if we just waited." And after about two minutes, we were shown into Mr. McLoughlin's office. I guess they didn't want Rosalynde and me sitting around there all day.

I had brought a portfolio of photographs I had taken, over the period of a year, of the New York City Ballet company, showing what their daily routine consisted of, and I explained that I wanted to do the same thing with the police. The deputy commissioner must have liked what he saw because he asked right away how long the job would take. Would an authorization for two weeks be enough?

Well, normally it would be, but I told him I didn't know how much time I'd have to put in on this job because of other jobs that might come in. I mentioned at the same time that I had already spoken with Gene and Brian, and so it wouldn't be like starting from scratch.

In the end, he signed an authorization—good for a year. And that was what we took to the Midtown South Precinct and registered with the people in the office upstairs. Gene and Brian wanted to know when we would be starting.

"Tomorrow night!"

And we did. And at the end of their tour, sometime around midnight, they asked if we were coming back the next night. Practically as a challenge.

"Sure. We're going to do this for a year."

They laughed. But we were there the next night—and every night, in fact, over the following two weeks. Still, they seemed to be challenging us.

"We know you're not going to come back *tomorrow* night. . . ."

But we did.

By then, the photos of the Monaco were a thing of the past—*Car and Driver* had run them, others were used for sales promotion by Dodge—but we now had a different subject: Midtown South. And we saw and heard many things there, mainly in the company of two New York police officers, two men with the rank of detective who had gold shields on their uniforms (signifying master patrolman) but who were still "out there," out on the midtown streets, two men proud of those uniforms and devoted to their beat, two men who turned out in shirts and ties even on summer days when the Manhattan temperature seemed like 104 degrees.

We learned a lot about New York and a lot about the police in the time we spent with Gene Gentile and Brian McMenamin. What follows is part of their story and ours.

Midtown South runs north and south for sixteen blocks—from 29th Street to 45th—and from Ninth Avenue over to Lexington. A high crime area. But unlike most other precincts in New York, it's made up of a lot of different and sometimes almost contradictory things.

Sex shops and massage parlors are massed around Times Square and 42nd Street, Seventh to Eighth Avenue ("the Apple"). The Precinct counts more than five churches and synagogues, plus the usual number of hospitals and fire houses. Shubert Alley is the heart of the New York theater district. The main public library and the main post office are in Midtown South, along with the garment and fur districts, Grand Central Station, Penn Station, the Port Authority Bus Terminal, any number of world-famous restaurants, plus some of the sleaziest hotels known to humanity.

Millions of shoppers flock to Macy's and Gimbels every year—just like the pickpockets and shoplifters that big stores always attract.

In Midtown South, there's the Pan Am Building, the Empire State Building, Madison Square Garden, the entrance to the Lincoln Tunnel—and every New Year's Eve, a big ball of light comes down in Times Square.

That's one event, on one night of the year.

That leaves the other three hundred and sixty-four. . . .

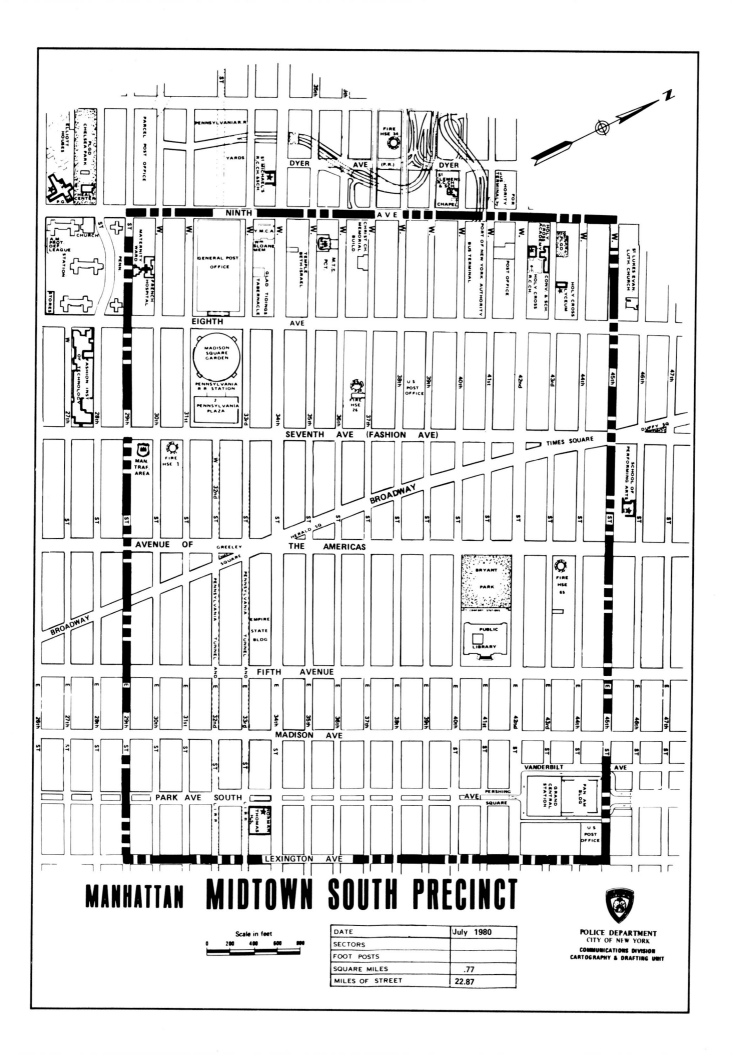

MANHATTAN MIDTOWN SOUTH PRECINCT

DATE	July 1980
SECTORS	
FOOT POSTS	
SQUARE MILES	.77
MILES OF STREET	22.87

Scale in feet
0   200   400   600   800

POLICE DEPARTMENT
CITY OF NEW YORK
COMMUNICATIONS DIVISION
CARTOGRAPHY & DRAFTING UNIT

The politician, the businessman, the commuter—they're going to have to realize that this is their city.

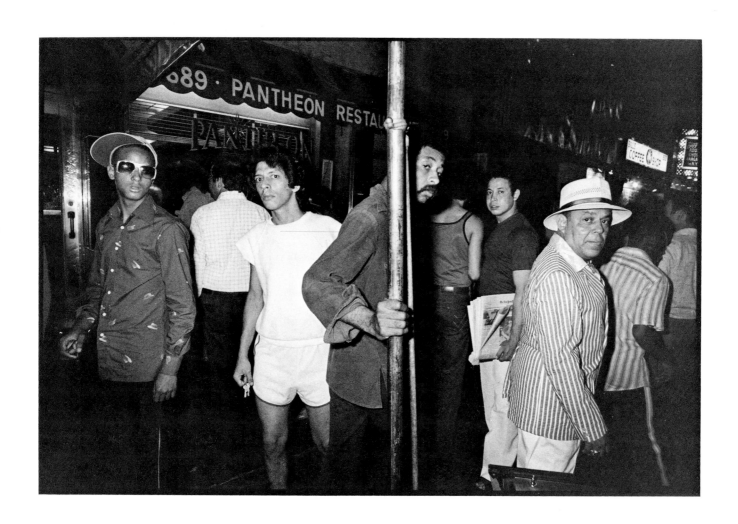

I was born in the Bronx on Fordham Road near Arthur Avenue. My father was a police officer. We lived on 183rd Street and Southern Boulevard. Then my father bought a house near Westchester Square, and we moved there.

When I was ten or eleven, I used to walk along my father's beat. It was his street and everybody knew him. I couldn't walk past the candy store or the grocery store without somebody coming out and saying, "Come in and have a Coke. . . . Have an egg cream with your father." Every person that lived there would come over and shake hands and say, "Is this your son, Andy?" Or they'd ask me, "Are you going to grow up and be a cop?"

In my neighborhood, there were mostly Italian and Irish kids, a couple of German kids. I was one of the only guys to go to a Catholic school. Because my parents wanted me to have a better education.

So I went to a Catholic high school. Then I left there and went to Christopher Columbus High School. All the guys I grew up with either went to jail or became policemen.

Later, I went to John Jay College. For one year. I didn't like it because of all the liberalism being taught.

After that, I worked in garages, I worked in the Botanical Gardens, things like that.

During the time I had a job in a gas station in the same precinct where my father had worked, people would come over and tell me things they remembered. Like the guy that had the candy store on the corner.

"These guys were in here bothering me. They were all drunk, and they ordered things and broke the glasses. Then I seen your father walking down the street, and I told him, 'Andy, these guys came in and they're giving me a lot of trouble. . . .' And the next thing you know, there's three guys laid out. I couldn't believe it. Nobody could believe it. He just kicked them on their ass and sent them on their way. And everybody was happy."

Not long after that, my father said, "Tomorrow is the test for the Police Department. Why don't you go take it?" I told him I didn't want to. "Go take it," he said. "I'll drive you over there."

So I took the test. And I forgot about it. Then, a couple of months later, they called me and said to come down and take a physical.

I passed the physical and went on to the Police Academy. After that, they gave me a uniform shirt and told me to go to the 30th Precinct and work.

So in 1967, I went to Harlem.

In the Bronx, I considered myself very street-wise. But I was like a fish out of water in Harlem. It was nothing in the world like the Bronx.

It was totally black. And this was a good Harlem precinct: Sugar Hill. It went from 141st Street to 165th Street on the West Side. It was where all the doctors and lawyers and congressmen would move. That was being a "fat man in Sugar Hill." When you were a fat man and you were making money, you'd move to Sugar Hill.

That was the 30th Precinct. It was a good house.

When I was a kid, I used to go down to 42nd Street a lot. I was about fifteen, and I'd go there with my friends—one guy was eighteen and he had a car. We used to go into the perv stores and look at the magazines. And like in those days, *Playboy* was a perv magazine.

Anyway, this one night, the guy in the store won't let me in. "You can't come in here, kid!" Now all my friends are in the store—and I'm standing outside. So I start walking toward Eighth Avenue and I get to the place where the holster store is now—four-two and eight—right by the subway.

So along comes a cop. "What are you doing here?"

Now what's the typical answer the nigger will give you every time? "I'm waiting for a friend," right? So I tell the cop, "I'm waiting for a friend."

Boom! He gives me a shot across the ass with the nightstick, throws me down the subway stairs, and says, "Go home! Get out of here!"

Now I was a city kid, but I hated the trains. I'd come downtown in a car—or not at all. So like if I'd tried to go home on the subway, I would've got lost.

Anyhow, I decided not to come to 42nd Street anymore. And I'd never again tell a cop I was "waiting for a friend." Because you know what he'd say to that? "Well, he ain't comin'!"

On my very first day in the Police Department, I sat at the switchboard. It was a Monday morning, and suddenly the door opens and this black woman comes crashing into the station house, screaming, hysterical, with blood coming out of her face. Very, very badly.

She runs over to me, falls on top of the desk, falls over my switchboard, and then bleeds all down the switchboard, all over the books. I say, "Hey, lady, get out of here." You know.

So the cops come over, and they sit her down. The lieutenant says, "Send for an ambulance." Now I didn't even know how to call for an ambulance—I was just a trainee at the time—but finally, an officer put in the call, and they took her away.

It turned out she'd been married for two weeks, and that morning, she burned the pancakes. Her husband didn't like it, and he took a fork and stabbed her in the face with it.

That night, I went home with blood all over my shirt—it wasn't mine—and my mother said, "What happened? You're not going back. You're not going to be a policeman. Your father's had enough of it. You're not going back."

I went back. And I had a lot of fun—because it was an enlightenment. You just wake up. People live in shells all their lives. Then, all of a sudden, you're here and this is the real world. This is what it's all about.

The first thing everybody wants to do when they come out of the Police Academy is get into a police car. Moving from a foot post into a radio car is like the difference between the infantry and the tank corps.

And the second thing they all want to do is become detectives. That's because in the news, in the entertainment media, the TV and the movies, cops don't do *anything*. It's the detectives that do everything. In reality, the backbone of the job is the cop that's out there in the street. He's doing everything. He's working.

When anything happens, it's the cop that goes there. It's nobody else. No boss, no ranking brass. Just cops and sergeants. Those are basically the only people that are out there. No lieutenants and captains are on patrol, picking up bombs, helping people when they're having babies and things like that. And that's what I enjoy.

Like tonight when those girls got ripped off. It's a satisfaction to do the right thing for someone who may go home and remember that maybe cops aren't bad. That maybe cops are good. Like, "Look, he gave me money to get home. He drove us back. He even left with a smile." Things like that.

Everybody turns to a cop when they need something. I just hope that people would remember times when they had a helper.

People who work in the Times Square area feel they have to be there. And tourists feel almost the same—imagine going to New York and not seeing Times Square.

A certain kind of excitement seems to be associated with Times Square—and has been for a long time. Today, it is generally believed that anything you want can be had in Times Square. Which is generally true. People who go there find that it is more than they'd expected. More dangerous, usually.

The first time I went out on post on 42nd Street, I couldn't believe it. It was worse than Harlem.

Now if you're going to be a bad guy, you're not going to be a bad guy in front of your own house. You're going to go somewhere else and be bad.

So they come to Times Square. All the bad guys from Harlem and Bedford-Stuyvesant, all the bad guys from Jersey and Connecticut come to Times Square eventually. They hang out, they act crazy, they do their thing.

When they go home, they can relax. But here, they feel they're in a war zone. They have to be tough guys.

You people are living in a bubble. People at home—whether they live in a better section of New York City or they live on Long Island or in Westchester—outside the Times Square area, they're in that bubble. They don't see what's going on. They only see what's on TV. And everything that's on TV and in the news is edited.

When I leave here, I too return to that bubble. I too go home. But I'm also out of the bubble. Every day. Right here in Midtown South.

I'm not saying that I know more than you. Let's just say I'm a little more street smart. And believe me, that bubble is going to break.

At one time, we had to guard the precincts—one man in front, one man in the back—because up in the Bronx, they'd found a stick of dynamite beside the gas pumps at the rear of the building. The BLA was doing a lot of that stuff.

So my assignment was to guard the back of the Precinct. I was a new guy, and the new guys would always get that—it was considered a shit assignment—because you just stand there all day long.

So I'm standing out there on 35th Street and I smell smoke. I look up, and there's flames coming out of this hotel, this real skel hotel. I don't have a portable radio because if you're only in the back, you don't really need one. Okay, I run down to the hotel and I tell the deskman to call the Fire Department. After that, I pull the fire alarm box inside the hotel. But unbeknownst to me, when you pull the fire alarm box inside a hotel, it only goes down to the desk and not to the Fire Department.

So now I run up the stairs to where the fire is and I see a room with all this smoke and shit coming out of it. And then a black guy comes stumbling out. I grab him and say, "Anybody else in there?"

"Yeah, yeah . . . Mickey's in there."

"All right, give me a hand getting him out."

"I'm not going back in there!"

"Give me a hand. . . ."

"You can't make me go back in there!"

So I get him by the neck, I choke him, and I haul him back into the room with me. In the bed is an old man. He's only got a pair of underwear on, and he's crippled with arthritis—big, swollen hands and knuckles. He's trying to get out of bed, but he can't—so I grab him and drag him out of the room.

I sit him down in the hallway—he's got tears in his eyes, he's an old skel—and while I'm doing this, the turkey runs away.

So now I see the fire hose. I pull it down off the wall and drag it into the room. Then I have to run back out in the hallway and turn the hose on. Just then, I hear the sirens of the fire engines. So I throw the water valve on—and the fire hose explodes! It was all rotted. And now I'm soaked.

Okay, the firemen come running up the stairs.

"What have you got?"

"I found this guy in the room . . ."

So they put the mask on him.

". . . but look. I'm soaked!"

The firemen could see the hose that had exploded.

"Yeah. Them hoses never work for shit. We cut 'em right off and put on our own."

We send the guy to the hospital and I go back to the Precinct. Now I never did anything that I wanted a pat on the back for, but what I'd just done is what you read about in the hero awards in *The Daily News*—and I wanted a pat on the back.

So I come up to the desk, I'm soaking wet, and I tell the sergeant, "I had station house security, there was a fire down at the corner and I just went in and put it out with the firemen. Then I sent the man I took out of the room to the hospital."

"Okay, don't worry about it. Nobody was looking for you. Go back on your post."

My first partner was Timmy Phelan. He was a seasoned veteran in Midtown South—he'd been there two weeks longer than I had.

Me and Timmy had a post on Eighth Avenue from 40th Street to 43rd. Both sides of the street including the Port Authority, plus a half-block on the streets going off Eighth Avenue. We had that post when we came on this job in the early 1970s. There was never a crime committed when we were working there that we didn't catch the guy who did it. Or prevent him from doing it.

When we got there the first day, me and Timmy fought all the way up the fucking street and all the way back down. Then we turned around and did it again.

There were decent stores all along the street. There was a Barracini's on one corner, there was a Fanny Farmer's further down. There was a couple of lingerie stores. The old ladies used to come out and say, "Oh, thank you." Now, there's nothing but shoeshines, parking lots, and junk stores.

We worked that post hard. The people knew us, the mutts knew us, everybody. We walked the post and it was our post. Nobody carried a bottle on Eighth Avenue, there were no holes out there blowing guys. We chased them away.

We were accountable for every person on that block. And we got the job done. Every day, round the clock, from 1970 until I went in the car with Brian in 1972 or so. Every day. I never wanted to take a day off. I came to work knowing it was my street and that no one was going to fuck with that street.

We ran that street with an iron fist. And it got easier and easier every day because the mutts would say, "Holy shit, here come the cops with the black gloves. Let's get out of here!" and they'd run away. This is my third pair of leather gloves. . . .

When we walked the post, the ground shook. And that's the way it should be. It will never get back to that again. Never, ever. We've lost too much. You think any cop is going to do that now? For what?

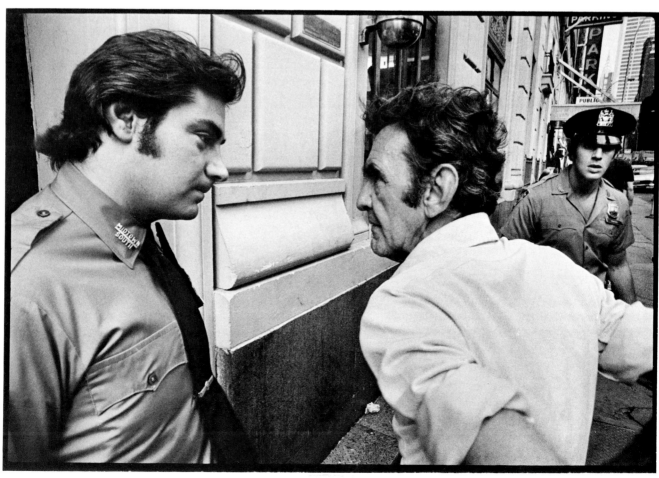

My partnership with Brian is more than a partnership. It's more like being brothers. I never had an older or a younger brother, and he lost his brother in a car accident before we became partners.

So I think we are closer than brothers. We're closer than husband and wife. Most partners become that way. You're with someone more than eight hours a day, sitting no farther than two feet apart. You do things together. There's monotony, there's tension. You have aggravation together and you have excitement together. All the excitement, all these emotions bond a friendship. And the friendship lasts forever.

And he's a very good partner. When we do things together, when we handle jobs and assignments, there's nothing we can't do. That's the way I feel about it. I know our capabilities and I don't know our limitations. Because we've never been anyplace that we couldn't do the job. We've never been anywhere that the job didn't get done.

We've never been hurt, physically hurt. And we've never been hurt through the Police Department. Nobody's ever said, "You did the wrong thing and we have to fine you a certain amount of time." Never. We've never had a problem with a boss, a sergeant, or any captain. They've always said, "You're good workers." They were always happy we were there. They want something done, you want something done, call us and we'll do it.

And the partnership works like machinery, well-oiled machinery. I know what he's about to do, he knows what I'm about to do. It works out fine. I never had an argument with Brian when it was like someone arguing with malice or hate, accusing or something. I never had any reason to. We argue over little things, trivial things. Because it takes the tension off.

For almost a year after he broke up with his wife, he lived in my house. He is as close to my wife and my children as an uncle or a brother would be. And the same way with myself and his children.

So it's like a marriage. When another police officer meets one of us and doesn't see the other one, he'll say, "What's going on? What are you doing without your partner?"

And it's an uneasy feeling to work with a different man every night because if something happens, you don't know if the guy will be there to back you up.

The night Gene and I made our first arrest, we were on a late tour—midnight to 8:00 A.M.—in May or June of 1972. We were filling out a report on a mugging when a call came in concerning a stabbing on Ninth Avenue and 36th Street. We ran out of the station house—and right into one of those situations that can really get you worked up, no matter how hardened you are. We found a pregnant woman lying on the sidewalk in a pool of blood. She'd gotten it right in the stomach.

While we were waiting for an ambulance, the woman described her assailant: "He's a black man, around six-two, and weighs about two hundred and fifty pounds. He's got on a yellow T-shirt, blue trousers, and sneakers." She said that he'd insisted on having sex with her, but because of her condition—and his size—she had refused. An argument started, and he stabbed her. She also told us he was staying at the YMCA on Ninth Avenue and 34th Street.

There was no ambulance available, so she was placed in an RMP that had responded to the call and was then taken to St. Clare's Hospital.

We went back to the station house to finish the report. Then, because it was close to our 3:30 meal period, I asked Gene if he wanted to go and eat—or go out and collar this creep. Of course, he was as eager as I. So we tried to work out where the guy would be. Or *wouldn't* be. Such as back at the YMCA, or at least not until "the heat was off." Or anyplace east of Ninth Avenue—too commercial and not enough places to hide. And if he had blood on his clothes like the woman said, he'd be trying to avoid people seeing him.

Okay, so the most likely area was between Ninth Avenue and the Hudson River, a couple blocks north or south of 36th Street. He'd last been seen going south on Ninth Avenue, so we decided to start on 34th Street and walk west.

BINGO! We hadn't walked more than two hundred feet when we found him. There were bloodstains on the front of his shirt—and he still had the knife in his hand. We both had our guns pointed right at his face—he wasn't more than six feet away—and Gene and I both had exactly the same idea: We oughta shoot this fucking animal. Anyway, before we arrested him and took him for identification, we made one thing very clear. "You stabbed a pregnant woman, you low-life motherfucker. If she dies—or if the baby dies—you're going for murder!"

When we got to St. Clare's, the woman identified him and we took him to the station house. At eight that morning, I put him on the "wagon." He went to court and was held on bail with his case scheduled for a hearing about six weeks later. Then I went before the Grand Jury where he was indicted for attempted murder.

I was in court the day the case came up. I could see the DA, the defense counsel, but no sign of the complainant or the perp.

And then was I surprised! Just as the case was called, in through the courtroom door walked the complainant, no longer pregnant, arm-in-arm with the guy that had stabbed her. She requested that all charges be dropped, the DA agreed, and they walked out just as they had walked in—arm-in-arm.

You learn to laugh in this job—the way I did as I walked out of court.

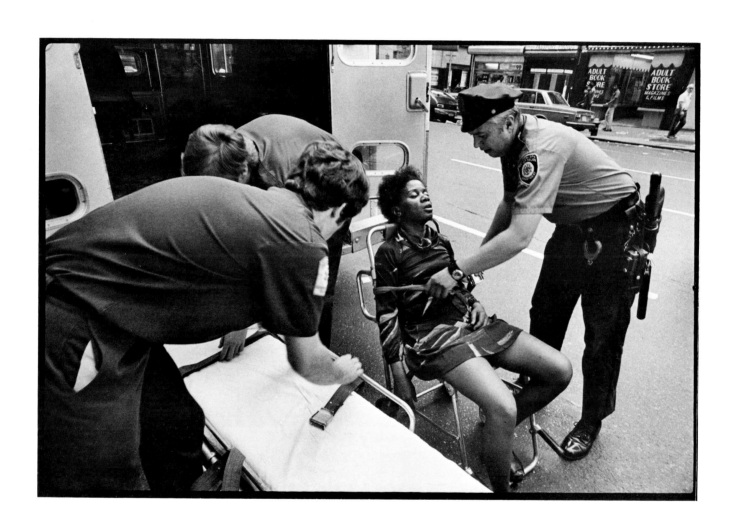

I will give up
MY GUN
when they pry
MY COLD DEAD FINGERS
from around it!

One time, the number of attacks on police officers increased greatly. These attacks were mostly by the BLA, the idea being to get guns away from policemen. And as often as not, the policemen were then summarily shot.

Gene and I worked out a routine for such situations that went like this: Suppose, for instance, he was threatened at gunpoint, and they told me to hand over my gun. First of all, I was sworn *not* to give it up, and second, I was to begin shooting on a prearranged signal. Immediately.

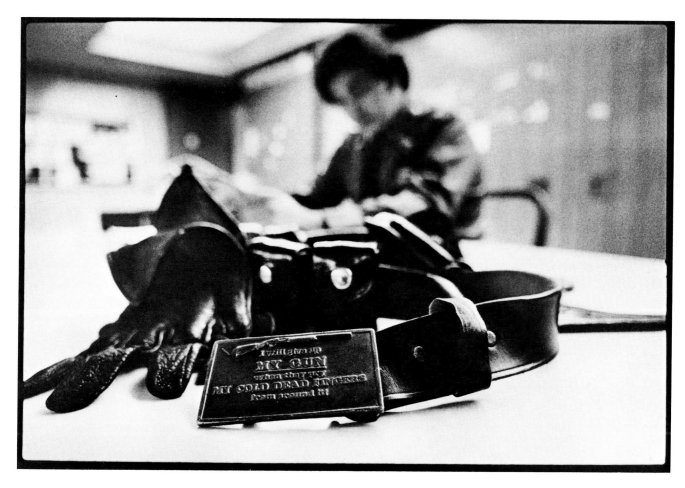

There was a period when there was a lot of assaults on policemen, guys getting shot left and right, all over the city. Me and Brian are in the car, it's about 4:20 in the afternoon, and all of a sudden, we hear a cop yelling into the radio, "Ten-thirteen! Ten-thirteen! . . ." That means that a cop is in trouble. "Shots fired! Shots fired!" And the cop yells the location—40th Street and Seventh Avenue.

Holy shit! Now you know it's a legit job. Here's a guy calling for help. He's telling you they're shooting at him.

We go cranking over there and come blasting down Seventh Avenue. "I'm in the substation!" That's a temporary police headquarters in a big mobile home parked in the street.

So we get there and jump out of the car. Now all the windows are punched out of the substation—and there's this guy laying there. So what happened is this: the guy went up into a building, up to the 44th floor, out on a window ledge and jumped. He came all the way out from the side of the building and hit the edge of the van, the substation that's parked there. He hit it with such force that it blew all the windows out. And the cop inside thought they were shooting the windows out on him.

Not only that, but when the guy hit the edge of the van, it ripped him wide open. So now, his intestines are stretched like about eleven feet into the street, into the lanes of traffic. Plus, he fell onto the subway grating in the sidewalk, so he's stuck there, jammed down onto the grating, and the shit is just oozing out of him down into the subway.

It's late now, it's almost five o'clock—so you got the intestine out into the street, cabs are going by, running over it, blowing their horns—and there's maybe two hundred people surrounding us, looking at this thing.

We get a sheet from the back of a radio car and throw it over the guy. And all the mutts are passing by, pushing those garment district racks and looking at the guy.

So we're standing there waiting for an ambulance. No ambulance. It's real busy, it might've been a Friday afternoon.

Now obviously the guy is dead after falling forty-four stories, and the people are crowding around closer and closer. They want to get a good look, right?

All of a sudden, we hear the rumble of a train underground. *Boom boom.* And the train goes by and a gust of wind blows up through the subway grating. And the sheet comes up—it looks like the guy's getting up.

So now you got people running in all directions, scooting every which way, yelling and screaming.

"Holy shit! Feet, don't fail me now!"

It was like rush hour and I'm at a foot post on 42nd and Eighth. I'm standing there watching the people when this Thunderbird comes up Eighth Avenue, goes right through the light, turns on 42nd, keeps going, and finally gets stuck in traffic.

So I go up to the guy. "Give me your driver's license and registration."

"What for?"

"You went through a red light."

"No, I didn't."

I give him a summons for passing the red light, and he says that he'll see me in court, that the only reason I gave him a summons is because he's black. Okay?

So we go to court and the judge says, "What happened, Officer?" I explain. Then the judge calls the guy to come forward. He's wearing beads around his neck, no shirt, a vest, short pants, sandals, and he's got a comb sticking out of his head.

He grabs the microphone they have in the courtroom and says, "I didn't do shit!"

The entire courtroom is laughing. Everybody is roaring.

The judge asks him what happened.

"I was driving, watching the people, and when they got out of the way, I made my turn and went on."

"Weren't you watching the lights?"

"No, I was watching the people. When they got out of the way, I just went through."

"Weren't you watching the lights?"

"No, I was just watching the people."

So, all right. Guilty. $25 please.

"I'll take this to the Supreme Court. I only got a summons because I'm black. You're a racist."

Okay, next case.

One day, there was a woman in the Port Authority. Unconscious. Overdose of drugs. She was very young looking. The ambulance was there, so we took her to the hospital.

Up at the hospital, she seemed to be okay. She was able to talk, so I said, "How do you feel?" She wouldn't give me her name or anything. "What's wrong?" She said, "I'm hungry." So I went downstairs and got her some coffee and a roll. I handed it to her and said, "Here, enjoy it."

I spoke to the doctor and the doctor said she was okay, she could go. Then, as she was putting on her coat, she pulled a gun out of her bra and put it in my stomach. "Okay, motherfucker, this is it!"

I looked down and saw it and said, "Holy shit, Timmy—it's a gun!"

And I watched her pull the trigger. And like the gun *didn't go off!*

So then Timmy grabbed her hand, I grabbed her other hand, and we got it away from her. And I arrested her.

It went to the Grand Jury—for no reason that we could see. Then we found out she was on parole from Baltimore. She'd stolen $1500 worth of guns from her father who was a gunsmith and gave them to some, like, Black Panther organization.

So in the Grand Jury, they held her for psychiatric observation because they thought she was crazy. And while she was being held, we found out that her boyfriend had shot a policeman in Brooklyn with a shotgun, and she was under the impression that we had known about it. You know, like "Wanted for . . ." We really didn't have any idea. We just figured she was an ordinary person who was sick and we tried to help her out.

She got six months in Bellevue Hospital. For "observation." And then they let her out.

Attempted murder . . .

Now any time a police officer takes a gun from a suspect, he has to go to Ballistics with it. They fire the gun to see if it's operative, and they check the bullets against any crimes that may have been committed with that caliber gun.

That's what happened when I brought in the gun I took from the girl in the hospital, the one she stuck in my stomach. The Ballistics officer took the gun into a room and fired it.

This time, it went off. And when it did, my stomach dropped to the floor.

Oh, man . . .

There's a magazine called *Law and Order*, and they had just come out with an article about a concealable bulletproof vest that you can wear underneath a uniform and that not many people would recognize.

What got me was the guy that designed the vest. He went to Detroit where there was a meeting of the PBA— that's the union—and said he was going to give a demonstration. There were about two hundred policemen standing there; I still have photographs of it.

So he got up on the stage, took out a .38 with a six-inch barrel—which is bigger than ours—and then he put it against his chest and fired.

Everybody was amazed. They thought the guy was crazy.

Then he lifted up the vest. Just a big black-and-blue mark. That was all.

Some demonstration.

Since then, I've worn one every day. This is the third one I've owned. They wear out from being wrapped against your body so tightly. They fray, the edges fray.

Every day. I wear that vest every day. But I wouldn't want that to get publicized.

If they know you've got a vest on, they'll shoot you in the head.

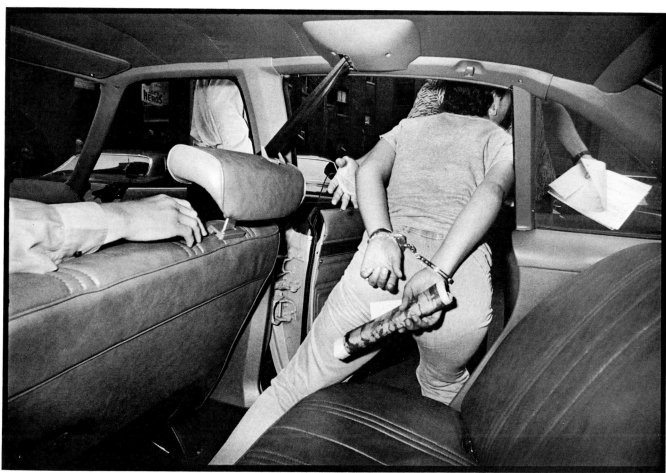

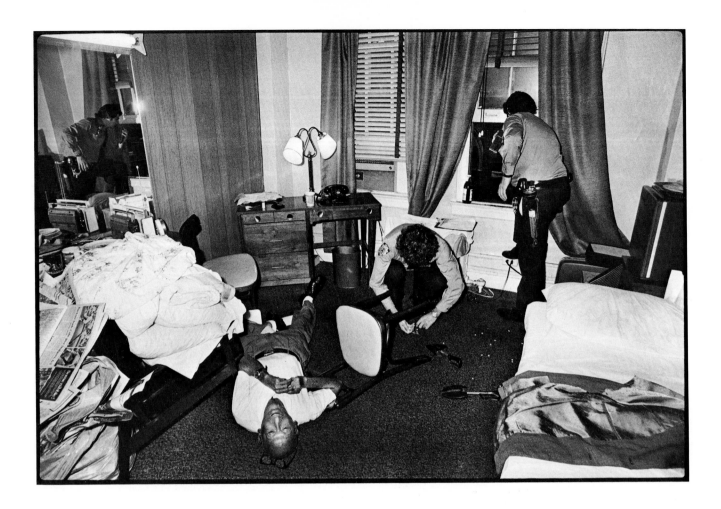

When somebody dies, there's invariably property to be settled. People who claim to be the next of kin can claim the property, but first they have to go through a municipal agency. Once it's confirmed that they are the next of kin, then they can come to the Precinct and claim the property.

So the first thing we do is search the body for personal effects, cash and that sort of thing. Then we look for insurance policies, bankbooks, jewelry—anything portable like radios or small TV sets. Everything that appears to be valuable has to be vouchered and taken to the Precinct and safeguarded.

Besides that, there's a primary investigation as to the cause of death. The first police officer on the scene will usually make a determination as to whether or not it appears to be natural. If it does, he'll just notify the medical examiner and the sergeant. If not, he'll also put in a request to Homicide, the detectives will come, and they will make that determination. We don't have the authority to declare a guy dead—even if he was blown up and has been dead for months. That's for the medical examiner to do. And after that, they send the meat wagon.

The worst DOAs are the old ones, the ones that have been dead a long time. Once you smell one, you'll never forget the odor as long as you live.

When a person dies, the muscles relax and everything in the bowels starts to flow out. That's why I carry plastic gloves in my briefcase. Because when we get one, we have to move the body around, straighten out the arms and legs, and look for wounds. I mean, if a guy's been hit by a train, we have to find out what goes where and put it all together.

When the ambulance comes, we have to go and deliver the body to the morgue. And we have to get a receipt.

Dying is not a very profound occurrence.

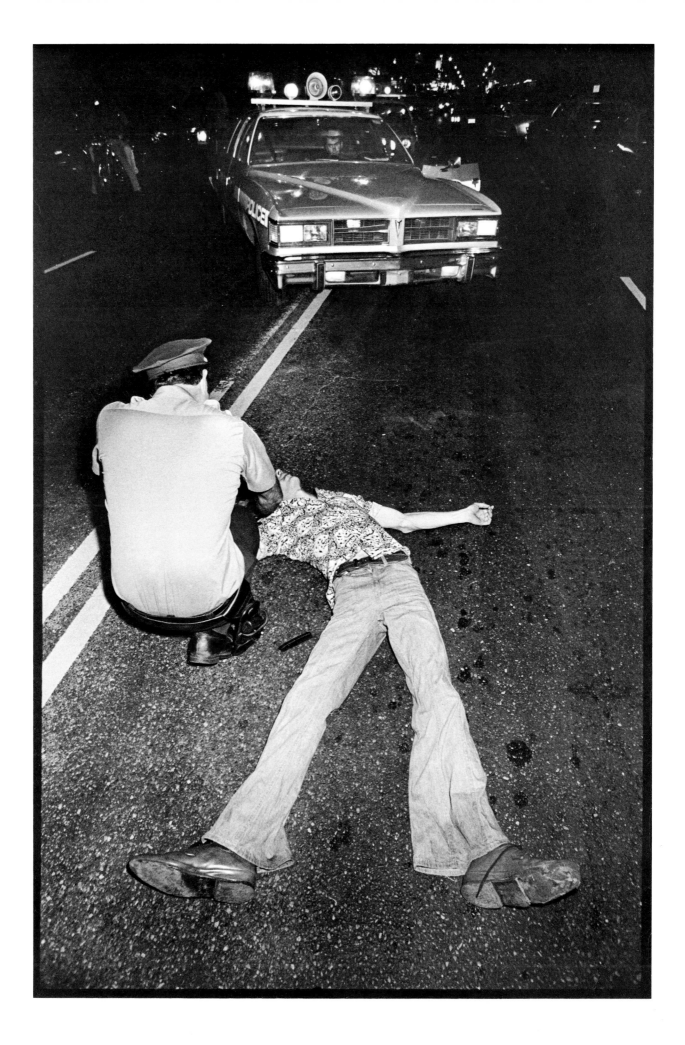

There was this sergeant I had a problem with, and so any DOA, any shit job he'd give to me. Like the worst DOA I ever had.

It's a Sunday afternoon about five and I have to go to 42nd Street and Ninth Avenue. It's a tenement and I walk all the way to the top floor. Now the door is broken off the hinges, and what happened was that people started smelling a dead body, and they called the police. The police ripped the door off to get in, and they couldn't get it back on.

I get in there and there's a woman laying on the bed. There's no sign of foul play, but there's roaches and bugs and flies and all kind of shit, all over the bed. It's summertime, it's hot, and the smell has got me around the throat. The last time anybody had seen her was about three weeks ago, so she could've been dead all that time.

I start playing with the door to get it to close. Finally I get it closed, but it won't lock. But now I have to get rid of the fucking smell. So I empty every bottle of perfume I can find into a saucepan and I boil it on the stove, just to make the stink go away. It wouldn't kill the stink. And burning coffee grounds and tea bags wouldn't either.

Now I know this sergeant is a ball buster so I've got to stay there with the body. There's a fire escape on 42nd Street, and I'm sitting there, waiting for the fucking ME. And it's getting dark now, and the only thing that works is one bulb in her room. That and the TV set—that only came in on Channel 2. Ed Sullivan was on, I can remember like it was yesterday.

Anyhow, I'm waiting for the sergeant or the meat wagon, and all of a sudden, I hear a knock on the door. I get up and I look over at the woman. Holy shit! I can see her eyes blinking.

I take my flashlight and I go over there and look closer. There are cockroaches on her eyes, and it's the shiny parts of their bodies that make it look like her eyes are blinking.

Then I go over to the door, I open it, and there's a priest standing there. The PRs in the place must have told him there's a dead body in the building.

"Someone die in here, Officer? Can I be of any help?"

"Yes—right over there."

So he takes a look at her, he smells her, and says, "Nothing I can do for her" and he's out the door and down the stairs.

After that, I waited until midnight when I was relieved. I never saw her taken away. And I'm glad I didn't.

We got up to this skel hotel on a 10-54—that's an injury call—and we find a dead guy on the 6th floor. So we're guarding the body while we're waiting for the meat wagon, and all of a sudden, we hear, "Help! Help! Fire!...." coming from the next floor.

We get up there and we find an apartment that's all on fire. And inside, there's a body, completely burned. We call the firemen, they come, and they put out the fire. And then they pull out the body. It's completely black. The hair's all gone, the genitals are gone—we don't know if it's a man or a woman.

Now, it turns out it's a woman—she's been raped, then stabbed, and then they set fire to her in her bed. So she's laying there on the floor, and she's been dead for at least an hour.

The lieutenant from the Fire Department calls over one of the firemen, and what does he say?

"Start mouth-to-mouth resuscitation on her...."

No captain, no boss in the police force would ever tell a cop to do that and expect it to be done.

We were somewhere in the lower end of the Precinct, and all of a sudden we hear this thing come over the air:

"Quick! Quick! Get an ambulance! We got a man here in an elevator, and he's yelling that he's had his legs decapitated."

We started laughing. We were laughing our asses off. I mean, I'm sure it was a shitty thing for the poor cop who was holding this guy in the elevator, you know, with his legs cut off—but the way it came over: "... legs decapitated!"

We pissed ourselves laughing.

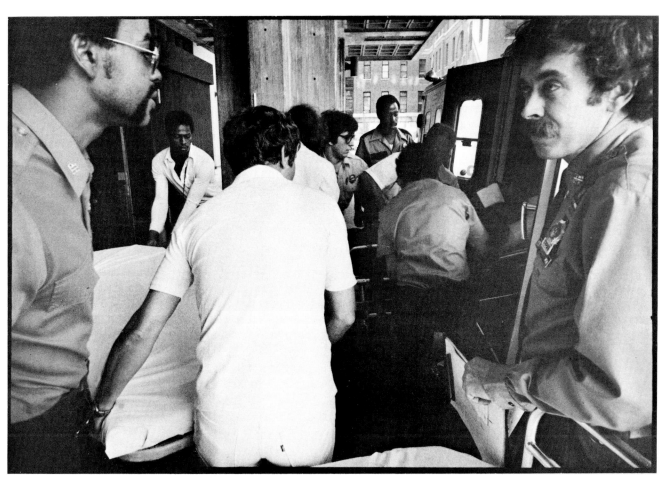

The sergeant says, "All right, Gene, you got a DOA up at the Commodore Hotel." So fine. I don't care, it's a job—I have to do eight hours. So I go up there, and it's a big, black woman, all swollen up. It's very hot and there's no air-conditioning on, so I go outside and Room Service comes by and says, "Hi, Officer. Is she dead?"

"Yeah, she's dead."

"Would you like something to eat?" Now I don't eat breakfast, but the woman comes back with coffee and some real loose scrambled eggs. I hate eggs. But she brought the stuff to help me. So I'm sitting there, waiting, waiting, and then Brian shows up with the sergeant. And then the meat wagon shows up. Everybody is up there on the 18th floor.

All of a sudden, they tell us that the Commodore employees just went on strike. So we're stuck up there on the 18th floor with this broad, and we can't get down in the elevator. One of the ghouls from the meat wagon asks me, "Where is it, Officer?"

"She's in there."

He takes a look at her and says, "We can't get her in the body bag. We're going to have to pop her head."

Now I've eaten the eggs anyway—because the woman brought them to me—and so by this time they're laying loose in my stomach, and I tell the guy, "Okay, but I'm going to wait outside. I don't want that shit splashing on me." All of a sudden, I hear like a watermelon falling on the floor. What the fuck was that? I look in the room, they got her shoved in the bag, she's ripped up the side of the bag, and splattered all over the pillow, all over the mattress. And now I can feel the eggs wiggling back up my throat.

Finally, we get some guy to run the elevator, and we can't get the body into it. Except standing up straight. So we're riding down in the elevator and all the shit is dripping down out of the bag. The doors open, we look out, and there's Channel 7 News, covering the strike. And here we are, carrying this body bag.

So now the hotel guy tells us we can't go out this way. And where does the guy take us so we don't get involved and see any people? Through Grand Central Station.

They had a homicide on a late tour. It turned out to be in our sector, so we had to go and guard the scene of the crime till the meat wagon came.

It was in the One Two Three Hotel right next door to G and G. We got up to the room and there was a white guy kneeling on the floor, his underwear down around his knees and he'd been stabbed twelve, fifteen times in the back. He was DOA in a kneeling position. Apparently some guy was balling him in the ass and got off just by stabbing him while he was doing him. "Not a very pretty one, is it?"

We closed the door and were sitting in the hall when a door opens up a little. There was this old woman, she must have heard us talking. She looked out, "Oh! The police!" She invited us in, her room was maybe six by nine, and that was her whole life.

She looked like one of the retired Times Square type people, one of them that never amounts to anything. Maybe, I don't know, show girl, dancer, what have you? Now she was in her sixties, living in this fleabag, run-down, welfare hotel, scared to go out of her room. Scared to even open the door for that matter. And only goes to the bathroom during the day because she's got to walk down the hall.

We must have been there, sitting and talking, in her room, a couple of hours—when we heard feet running back and forth upstairs. All of a sudden, shouts: "Fire! Fire!" So we run upstairs and sure enough there was a fire in a room. We got the door opened. There were flames, smoke, shooting out. The firemen came with the hoses and did the whole thing. They pulled out what was obviously a white female. She was completely naked, all her hair was burned off, she looked like a poached fish. They tried to do a mouth to mouth. The chick didn't make it.

Some of the local bullshit in the hotel was that she just came back from prison, and she had given up a few people to make her sentence a little easier. So they killed her and set the room on fire. They wanted to make it look like she had died smoking in bed.

The cause of death was that she had been given an overdose, "a hot load." (We knew one guy who got a hot load—he was in the hospital for over six months really climbing the walls.)

So there we were, sitting in the hotel with two DOAs. Two homicides, one on top of the other.

Brian was off that day. He had to go to court. So I'm working with another guy. A guy I won't name.

"Robbery in progress in a liquor store on Twenty-ninth and Ninth . . ."

We're at 45th Street, so I wheel the car down there. There's maybe six radio cars in front of the place already. A guy comes out of the store. "They robbed the cash register, they took my money, and they took my watch. And two bottles of Wild Turkey."

"Where did they go?"

"Around the corner. Into that building."

I turn to the guy I'm with. "Let's go."

"Oh, no, we have to wait for more help." The guy is, like, an inside man that I happened to get strapped with. But how much help do we need? There's six fucking radio cars right there.

"I'm going in. Anybody want to come with me?"

So this guy Greg Lettieri—he's out now—says, "I'll go with you, Gene."

Now these guys are supposed to be armed with a shotgun and knives and shit. Three black guys. We go into the building and we find the super. "See any guys come in here?"

"Yeah, I just seen a couple of black guys run up the stairs. Into Four-D."

We go upstairs and get on the radio to Emergency Service. Because they have the big vests, they have the heavy artillery. "Possible suspects in Apartment Four-D, armed with a shotgun."

So now I'm on one side of the door and Greg is in another doorway and we're waiting. Just then, the door opens, and a black guy and a white chick come out. We grab them and drag them down a flight of stairs. "What's going on in there?"

"Nobody's in there."

"Don't bullshit me."

"I swear, there's nobody in there."

"Okay, let's go back."

As we get to the door, I'm using the guy as a shield and Greg has the broad as a shield. I kick the door and throw the guy in.

It's a real small room. The closet door is open about three inches and I can see a black hand inside. So I put my flashlight in my left hand, pull out my gun, and yank the door open. Three mutts.

"Put up your hands, you motherfuckers!"

They put up their hands. Two of them start coming out and the last one reaches up to grab the shotgun that's on the top shelf of the closet. I can't get a shot at him because the first two guys are in the way. So I push them aside and start whacking the other guy with my flashlight.

Now they jump on us. All five of them. We're going round and round and I finally manage to wrestle the shotgun away from them.

They resisted pretty bad. I think Greg bent the bottom of his gun. There was a lot of blood. We get them laid out on the floor and I'm cuffing one guy to another guy—we only have three sets of cuffs between us.

Then Emergency Service shows up. They come in with the shotguns and machine guns. "What've you got?"

So I show the guy the shotgun, the Wild Turkey, and everything.

"Do you want the arrest?"

He wants to know if we'd like to give it away. After working our asses off.

Now it happened that one of the mutts' names was Clayton Jiggets. And we had this new captain at the time, and of course he's heard all about the arrests. But he doesn't know me from Adam.

So the next day at roll call, he gets up and says, "Fellows, I'll just take a moment of your time to mention the excellent arrest made last night by Officer Jiggets."

Aw, shit . . .

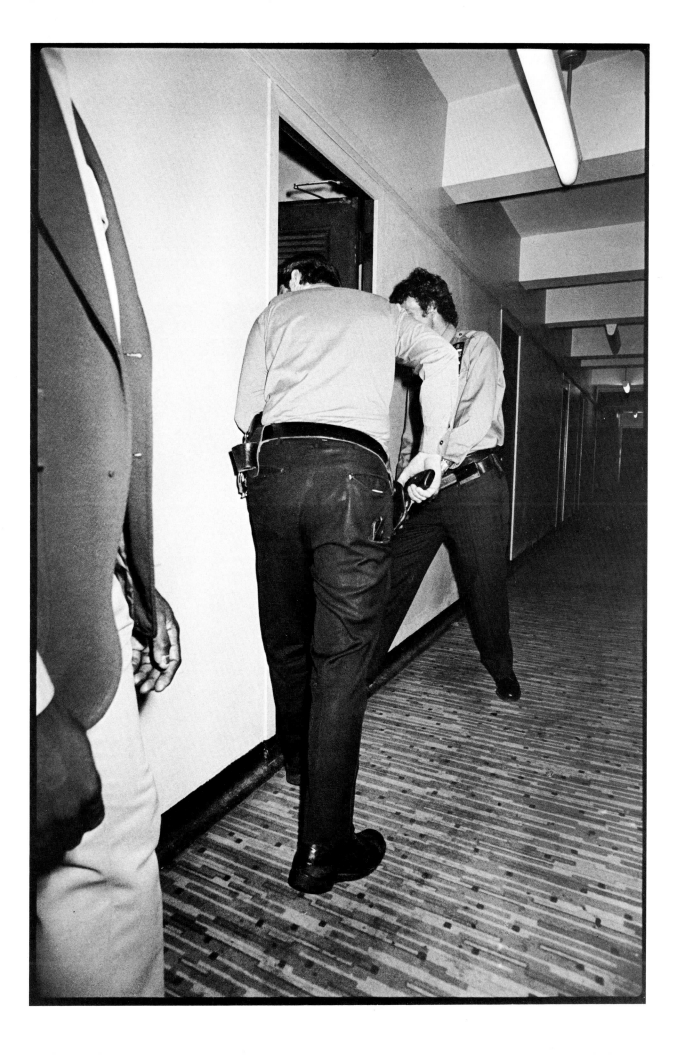

A little girl was brought into the Precinct by a cop. She was about thirteen years old, and the cop thought she was a runaway. We started to talk to her. She was reluctant to say anything, but after a while, we convinced her that we weren't the bogeyman.

She said she had run away and that she was ready to go back to Minnesota or Wyoming or wherever the hell it was. And she said she was staying in this particular place on Tenth Avenue, that this guy had picked her up in the Port Authority and brought her there. And now all she wanted to do was to get her schoolbooks back. She said, "I have to get my schoolbooks." That's how the human mind works—she was concerned about her schoolbooks.

On the way over there in the radio car, Brian tried to get her to open up a little. He told her the guy might have a dose. Then she became frightened and told us how this guy had raped her and so forth and so on. She described him as a light-colored guy, a Spanish guy, and she brought us to the apartment.

When we got there, we knocked on the door and we heard some scrambling around. Eventually, we got inside and we found this fellow who had a little boy in there, about nine or ten years old. We talked to the boy, and he told us that this guy had taken him off the street also, that he had him up in the apartment and he was fucking him in the ass. And he had all his friends over there, fucking him in the ass, turning him out.

There you have a guy who is legally an animal, you know, a dog. One sniff and he says, "That's for me." And it doesn't matter if it's male or female.

Needless to say, when we attempted to arrest this guy, he got out of hand. He was subdued easily and we wound up making the collar. And we got a medal out of it too, an EPD, an Excellent Police Duty. For taking this animal off the street.

A few years ago, all the guys in the Precinct were given a ballot when they got their checks on payday. It said, "Who do you think deserves extra compensation for the work he does out there on the street?" So each cop voted, and they compiled a list. And then the administrative lieutenant called us into the office. "You two were picked out of everybody to be promoted to detective, third grade. You'll get extra compensation—but for that extra compensation, you have to be training officers."

"What does that mean? What do we have to do?"

"You'll go train other cops."

"We aren't training anybody."

"You're turning down the promotion?"

"We don't want it."

"It's unheard of that a man gets a promotion and turns it down."

"Look, just leave us alone in Sector Adam. We'll drive around, doing the same thing we always do, and have a good time."

"If you don't take this, you get nothing."

"That's OK—we get nothing."

A little while later, another ballot came out—because at the time, the police commissioner said he wanted to compensate certain officers for a job well done, that certain men out there should be made master patrolmen. "Super Cops." It meant two stripes on your arm. So now the other uniformed services—the firemen and the garbagemen—said, "Well, if they have a Super Cop, we want a Super Fireman and a Super Garbageman." This had to do with parity and all that shit. But what the fuck does a garbageman do out there to deserve extra compensation? Whistle with no hands while he's picking up a garbage pail, maybe? Anyway, when all the furor and all the bullshit died down, they voted. And on December 23, 1973, we got our gold shields as master patrolmen . . . out on the beat.

Our radios pick up the messages for two other precincts, and one afternoon, we heard a Midtown North call requesting additional units for "a psycho with a knife" on Eighth Avenue at about 47th Street. We were just a couple of blocks away, so we decided to respond.

When we arrived at the address given, we were met by a very excited cop who explained that there was a guy on the 4th floor landing with a big knife holding about ten cops at bay on the floor below and threatening to kill the first one that came up the stairs. There was also something said about a woman and a child being held hostage.

We went up to the roof of the building next door, hoping to come down on the psycho. The door on the roof was locked, and while the other cops who'd arrived there too tried to break open the door, I motioned to Gene to follow me down the fire escape. I wasn't quite sure what we'd be able to do—but there wasn't much else that was working.

When we got to the 4th floor, I looked in a window. It was a kitchen—I could see a baby's bottle in a pot of boiling water on the stove.

I remember being concerned that there might be a dog in the apartment; I had been bitten by a dog once before, so I was reluctant to just step into the apartment. The window was partially open, so I raised it the rest of the way, as quietly as I could. I asked very softly if there was anyone in there—I figured if there had been a dog inside, he would have heard me. Nothing.

I stepped into the kitchen, turning off the gas under the boiling water as I moved toward the door. I could now hear a male voice yelling from somewhere beyond it and it was obvious that the psycho was out there. The door jamb had been split away from the frame, and peering through the space, I spotted the psycho, still yelling, on the top stair, looking down at a group of cops.

It would have been simple to just open the door a little and blow the guy away. However, during one of our training sessions, I had been surprised to learn that bullets don't ricochet the way that is generally believed. When hitting a wall, they tend to travel along it. So considering our angle of fire and the location of the psycho, it would be very likely that a missed shot would hit the wall and travel down toward our guys on the floor below.

I suggested to Gene that he contact the radio dispatcher and request that the officers on the landing move away and preferably go down to the second floor. But our portable wouldn't transmit from inside the building, and when he tried to call on the telephone in the kitchen, he couldn't get through.

Our only alternative then was to jump the psycho—who was yelling louder than ever. He appeared to be about six feet tall and heavyset, and was holding a large screwdriver about sixteen inches long in his right hand. Although it wasn't a knife as we had heard earlier, the screwdriver was still a very dangerous item. Under the best of circumstances, this guy was not going to be easy to take—it was imperative that we surprise him.

I told Gene that I was going to concentrate on securing the screwdriver and that he would have to immobilize the rest of him. On three.

One! Two! Three! And out the door!

We both lunged for the guy, and Gene's usual shouting had the usual effect of making him think that two wild men were about to dismember him. For a brief moment, he changed from the aggressor to the bewildered— and that was all it took. I got both my hands around his right wrist and Gene grabbed his legs.

The psycho went down, the yelling stopped, and the other cops rushed up the stairs. By now, I've got the guy handcuffed, and if they hadn't been my cuffs, we would've just left. I mean, when you go into another precinct, you go there to help out, not to interfere. Okay, so we did something these other cops couldn't do, we took this guy out. But when they asked, "Do you guys want it?"—meaning the collar, which would've been a big medal because of the hostage situation, the nonshooting arrest and all that—we just told them, "No, we only came to help."

There's always bosses. Take, for instance, this one commander we had. One night, we're all down at Madison Square Garden. "The Fruit of Islam"—Black Muslims, right?—are having this big rally there, and our commander comes over and says, "Look, these are very peaceful people, so we don't want any incidents here. If there's any trouble, call me. Even if there's a ten-thirteen, nobody goes inside."

And I'm thinking, Oh yeah? If there's a 13 in there, we're going! These "very peaceful people" have already killed two cops I knew personally.

So then he tells me to go outside. Which I do. And what do I see? A peddler. And he's selling Dixie Peach, all that shit. So I tell him, "Give me some kind of identification. . . ."

"What are you trying to do, cause a problem here?"

Now this isn't the peddler talking—it's the CO. Who then says, "Go out and direct traffic!"

Okay. So I go. I get my summons book out and what do I hear? The CO. "What are you doing?"

"These cars are triple-parked. How can I direct traffic when—?"

"You're really trying to cause an incident, aren't you? Maybe we're going to have a problem with you. Go inside. . . . You'll be Temporary headquarters now."

So I go inside, and it's like this: "I just got robbed. . . ." "They took my handbag. . . ."

Very peaceful people . . .

And what do I wind up with? A stack of 61s—and I hate to do reports. But I do them.

And then, right after that when we come back for a late tour, what's going on?

The pro-Communist Cubans and the anti-Communist Cubans are all over at the Manhattan Center—and we've got to keep them apart. So we go out, "hats and bats"—that means "helmets and nightsticks." We pull up, helmets, nightsticks, black gloves, and flashlights—and who do we see? The commander. And what does he want to know? "Which ones are the Communists here?" That's his only question.

Anyway, right then he tells us, "We don't need you guys. Get out there. Go back on patrol."

So we go. And by now, we're the only Midtown cops that aren't down there with the Communists. And all of a sudden, the radio goes crazy.

"Available South units for rioting and looting on 42nd Street."

Available? Sure . . . all two of us!

Okay, we go wheeling up there, and when we get to 42nd Street, they're breaking windows and taking stuff out. Eating the place alive. Now at that time, we're the only car there. Not another car in sight. It's a looter's paradise. People are running all over with TV sets and radios under their arms. So we drive up on the sidewalk with the lights and the siren on, the car doors open, and go right up and down the sidewalk. It's the only thing we can do. We sure aren't going to *arrest* anybody.

A half hour later, there's still just the two of us. We'd called for backup—"Whatever you got, we'll take. . . ." And who comes up? Our CO—in the back of a sergeant's car. And he looks around and says to the sergeant, "Maybe we ought to put Division on alert and get some men in here."

"Inspector," the sergeant says to him, "can I make a suggestion? Get all the bosses out of here, leave the cops alone, and they'll take care of everything." And that's just what happened. The CO went away, and by the time the sergeant got back, we've got maybe eight or ten cops there and we're really kicking ass.

Now there's this white guy standing there, stewed, I guess. Standing on the corner. And we're telling everybody, "Get the fuck off the street! Get out of here! Go home!" And this guy just stands there, looking at me. *Boom.* I hit him. He goes down, and I start kicking him down in the street. And then, somebody says something to me. I turn around, and there's a fucking captain standing behind me.

Holy shit! I don't even know this guy. But the captain turns to the guy on the ground. "Hello. Can I help you up? Did you fall down?" And the captain goes *boom.* "The officer told you to leave, cocksucker!" And I have no idea where this captain came from—he wasn't from our Precinct.

And that was it. We just wiped out the whole place. All you could see was assholes and elbows running down the street. Assholes and elbows.

We were on a foot post on Eighth Avenue and we get a 10-13—a policeman in danger. We jump in the nearest cab and tell the driver, "Get to 42nd Street—quick!"

The guy turns around, sees we're both cops, and asks, "Is this for real?" We tell him it is, and so then what does he do? He leans down under the dashboard and pulls out a siren. He hits the gas, burning rubber, and we go blasting uptown. The siren is wailing, and the guy is going through all the red lights.

"No! Don't go through the lights!"

He keeps right on going, and over the noise his siren is making, he yells, "Look—I've been waiting for this for twenty years!"

"Warning: If you value your own life as much as I value this bike, don't fuck with it." (Inscription on Gene's motorcycle.)

The parallel between the police and the Hell's Angels is that in the Angels' bylaws, in their constitution—and they do have laws they have to abide by—the main principle is that if one member engages in an altercation with a nonmember, all the other Angels who are present must participate. Let's say me and Brian are Angels and we're in a bar and he gets into a fight with some guy. Once the fight begins, I have to rat-pack the guy right along with Brian. That's to show the guy you don't fuck with motorcyclists because you're going to get your ass kicked.

In the same way, if me and Brian are out in the street and he gets into a fight with a perp, we're both going to do the guy in. That's so the perp will know you don't fuck with the police. Because you're going to lose. You may win one-on-one, but you're going to lose eventually.

The Hell's Angels know that if they fuck with the police, they're going to lose. They may have 1,000 members, but we have 30,000. So they're going to lose.

These two cops arrived in a radio car in Bedford-Stuyvesant, responding to a job: *"Burglary in progress. Possibly people armed with a gun."*

They went there, into a basement, and started searching. A dark basement at night with no lights on, okay? With flashlights, they found some people there. Teenagers. Then they went into another room. There was a guy there, all by himself, holding something in his hand. Looked like a gun.

One of the cops said, "Police. Don't move!" The guy turned around, spun around with the gun. *Bang.* The cop shot him. The guy fell down on the floor. Now what he had was a saw, a wooden-handled saw with a long, narrow blade on it. But in the dark, it could've looked like a gun. The cop had told him, "Don't move!" And the guy spun around. The cop killed him.

The cop was called before the Grand Jury. And the Grand Jury indicted him. He went to court—because of political pressure from the turkeys, all right? "Police officer kills a guy in the line of duty." They said it was murder.

In court, he was acquitted of murder, OK? But the Police Department says, "You're crazy. We don't want you anymore."

They gave him his pension, took away his guns, and told him to get off the job. They made him a psycho. He's a psycho now. They said he's unfit for duty, he's crazy.

When you shoot someone, you go before the Civilian Complaint Review Board. The board is composed of civilians and cops, bosses who haven't been out in the street for the past ten or fifteen years. They don't know what's involved, and they'll second-guess you every time. Monday morning quarterbacks.

In the case of the cop who killed the guy with the saw, the trial commissioner held a departmental trial—which is worse than any trial in court. Because it's a kangaroo court. Everything is accepted—hearsay evidence, everything. It's like a court-martial.

Now the person who has the ultimate say is the police commissioner. And the police commissioner never turns around anything the trial commissioner says. The police commissioner will appoint someone who'll say exactly what he wants said. He'll tell the trial commissioner, "I want this guy buried," and the trial commissioner will bury him. And that's it.

Only a couple of years ago, most cops felt that they'd rather be "tried by twelve than carried by six." That is, a cop would rather go to court and say to twelve decent people, "Listen, this is what happened," than be carried by six pallbearers.

Cops don't feel that way anymore. Today, they crucify you for doing something they think is wrong.

So maybe some guy is armed with a knife, and another guy is armed with a gun. It's the same type of thing that travels through your mind: After you've done something you're justified in doing, they start building a cross for you. And then you'll go through the problem. Your wife will go through the problem. And so will your family.

There you are: Trigger-happy, racist cop . . .

Makes good copy.

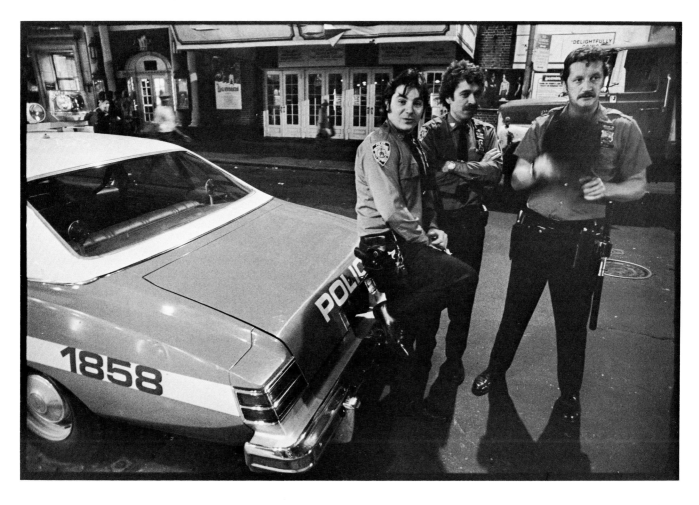

One of the things that's bad about this job is that departmental procedures are handled a lot different than they would be in court. When an investigation starts—whether it be a shooting investigation or a shakedown investigation or whatever—at one point, *one man* is going to make the decision whether the particular cop involved is right or wrong. And once that decision is made, the Department is going to build its case. Based on that one man's decision. And then the Department will go out and prove that particular conclusion.

They don't get proof and then draw a conclusion from the proof. They get a conclusion and draw the proof from the conclusion.

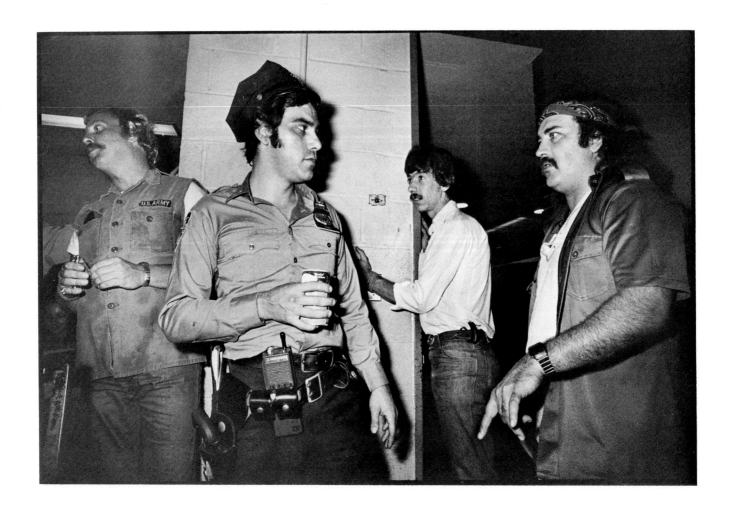

There was this one cop who was involved in a shooting. He was exonerated completely—but his chief didn't like him. "Fuck him. Transfer him."

And he was. At the whim of some pencil pusher or some guy who smokes a pipe in some ivory tower and hasn't been out there in the fucking street in twenty years.

It seems that now, on the midnight tours, maybe ten or fifteen of the Puerto Ricans or blacks on 42nd Street between Seventh and Eighth Avenues will jump on a guy, some white guy walking down the street, and punch him around, kick him, rip his clothes off, rip the chains from around his neck.

So this old man, who's got half a load on, is walking across 42nd Street. I'd guess he was in his sixties. The Wild Dogs of the Deuce get a sniff of him, and they start following him. In the middle of the block, they jump him. They take his money, his watch, his ring. Then they knock him to the ground, and while he's down there, they kick him all over his body, particularly his head.

This guy was beat up so bad—he was bleeding from his eyes, from his nose—that when we got on the scene, we thought he'd been hit by a car. That's how serious the injuries were.

That was the night we cleared the sidewalks. Cleared them better than if we'd used a flamethrower. We declared a police state on 42nd Street. Everybody was sent home or wherever.

There was no arrest made, but there were a couple of beatings administered. That's called bending the rules, the rules the bad guys don't play by.

There's no Marquis of Queensberry out there on the street.

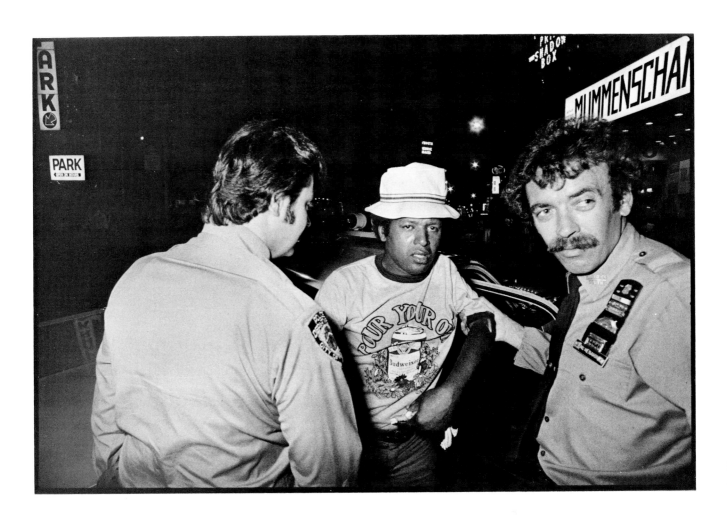

Take a place like Florida. My parents live down there, and one day three guys held up a supermarket. Two guys were killed outright and the other guy was wounded.

And the people just couldn't say enough; they went down to the little station house there, they donated money to the PAL and all. People feel safe when police officers use force.

But somehow it's gotten all twisted around. We just can't protect the decent people in this city the way we used to. It's sad, really.

It's hell trying to be a policeman in a liberal city. And it's not going to change until people's ideas on things change. It's not only us, it's the courts and everything else. Being a cop in New York is one of the roughest jobs in the world.

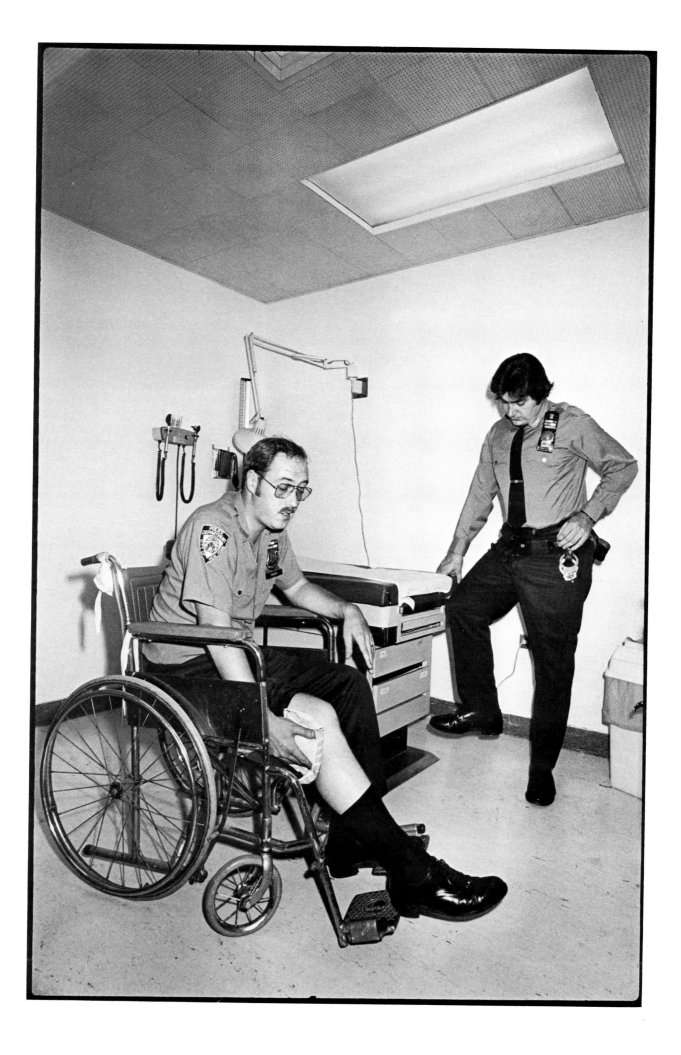

Over the years, I've been given a lot of verbal abuse and heard a lot of foul language. But a New York State Supreme Court judge said that police officers in New York City should have tougher skin than other citizens.

One day we're out there and we see this black couple come running out of Macy's. And right behind them is a guy who works for the store, chasing them. Up in front of us is a cop on a scooter, and he starts out after them. By the time we catch up with them, the couple has handed off whatever it was they stole in Macy's to some other guy who disappears immediately.

Okay, so here's Gene standing there with the two perps—who by now are absolutely clean. And the woman is shouting at him: "What kinda shit is this? What are you hassling us for, Pig? Why aren't you out catching murderers?"

Naturally, a crowd is starting to gather. And this is what they hear: "Look, you blue-eyed honky mother-fucker—you're nothing but a killer. I bet it's *you* who's the Son of Sam."

And this kind of abuse goes on and on. With Gene just standing there. Smiling.

After a while, this black lady from the Caribbean comes over to us and says, "Aren't you going to do anything?"

"What do you mean?"

"Aren't you policemen going to lock her up?"

"No."

"I come from Jamaica, and in my country, she'd get put in jail for doing such a thing on the street. You can't talk to a policeman like that."

Oh, yeah? Welcome to New York City, lady . . .

When my father retired, they had this big party. And one guy got up and said, "I remember Andy when I was a rookie. He took very good care of me. And if ever you wanted somebody knocked out, you called Big Andy—because when he knocked them out, they stayed out."

So everybody got up and cheered. I felt very good.

Then another guy came over to me and said, "I'm a detective today because your father gave me the arrest." The collar my father had given him was good enough to be some kind of news item. But they turned around and made the other guy a detective instead of my father.

"You've got big shoes to fill," he said. "Your father is like the dinosaur. There just ain't any around anymore. Once, they ruled the earth—and now they're all gone. The old-time cops are all gone. The bull cop would go out and he'd do the job. Everybody knew him. The decent people loved him."

He was right. But today, nobody appreciates the cop. They take cops for granted. And no cop is going to go out there and bust his ass for people who don't give a shit.

No mayor is going to come up and say that the answer to New York City's problems is having the cops go out and kick ass. No one has the balls to say that.

And the cops are not going to go out there and say, "Okay, let's beat the shit out of these motherfuckers." No, they're going to go out there and walk their posts.

I used to work in the Four-One Precinct in the South Bronx, better known as Fort Apache. That's where the medals come from. From the Fort. The green one is called the Combat Cross.

That lasted two years until the fiscal crisis required the city to lay me off. Today, I'm rehired and I'm in the Midtown South Precinct.

Once you're laid off, it's hard to get a job. Nobody wants to invest time and money in you because they feel you might get rehired as a cop at any moment.

Since it was two years before we got rehired, a lot of us had to take nonmeaningful jobs such as painting, security guard jobs at $3.50, $4.00 an hour, anything. Anything you could get your hands on, you took. Besides the security job, I worked weekends as a bartender for a catering outfit. I also collected money out of washing machines in South Brooklyn. It wasn't easy but you had to do it. To pay the rent.

I never made plans for another career. This is the only kind of work I wanted to do. And at thirty years old, it's kind of rough to start a new career. I already had two and a half years in the Department.

During this time, the PBA funded us—for a month, a fucking month. And then they dropped us.

I suppose I am bitter to a degree. But who am I going to blame? The mayor? Other cops? The city? I don't feel bitter toward anyone personally—I feel bitter because I was laid off for political reasons. It wasn't just one person who did it. Mayor Beame was a big part of it. But he wasn't alone.

It was a political move. I just don't believe that the city was in so bad a condition they had to fire cops. How many times did they nearly go bankrupt—and then an hour before, suddenly, miraculously, they found millions of dollars?

Evidently no one cares about laid-off police officers. But next time some guy is swinging a club at you, call someone at the Welfare Department or at the Sanitation Department or call a fireman—and see what kind of satisfaction you get.

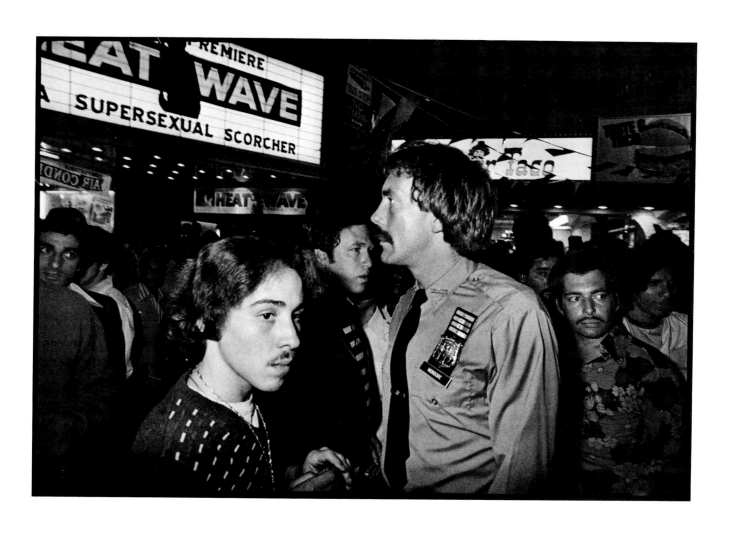

We never went on strike. We can't strike.

We're damned whatever we do. If we go out and bang the balls off the city with summonses, we're hurting the middle-class guy, not the politician upstairs. He's riding around with a fucking chauffeur.

Either you want to become a cop or you don't. And if you do, you have to put up with whatever they give you.

A cop is able to help people. He's able to do a lot of things that are beneficial. It's self-satisfaction. If you help someone off the floor, if that person is bleeding or sick, it's the personal gratification you get.

There's also the element of excitement. Adrenaline pumping. If you're worried about danger, you shouldn't take the job. Sure, I've used a gun a few times. That's how I got my Combat Cross. In a robbery. Me or him. He was pointing a shotgun at me from about eight feet away. He'd already fired twice, so there was no thought of, you know, "Does this man have a family?" If he's going to shoot at a police officer in uniform, then he deserves what he gets. It didn't do a thing to me.

Nobody told these people to go and buy a gun. If they'd gone out and got an education, whatever it might have been, then got a decent job and stuck to it, maybe they would have turned out like any other law-abiding citizen. But they took the short way: Buy a gun, rob a store, and now you got spending money. . . .

I've never got a complaint in this job from any boss, okay? No sergeant, no lieutenant, no captain has ever said to me, "You did something wrong, I'm docking you five days' pay." Never.

The Civilian Complaint Review Board has never charged me with a crime, assault, or anything like that. But they could. The DA's office could charge me with a crime.

I'm afraid to be as aggressive as I was before, but when I see scumbags like I saw today, inside of me I want to cut their legs off and throw them in the river—so that nobody has to look at them, no decent people, no regular people. I don't want people to have their senses assaulted by the shit that's laying in the street, the guy with his pants down, pissing in his pants, shooting himself, the other guy sucking a fucking jug. I don't want people to think that at any moment some jackal is going to jump on them and fuck them up. But how do you stop it?

There's other guys besides me and Brian out there doing it. Moving the mutts and things like that. But there's no reason to do it, there's no law that says you should.

There used to be. Public intoxication was a crime, loitering was a crime, obstructing the sidewalk was a crime, vagrancy was a crime. We used to lock people up for that.

What would they get? Nothing. They'd get nothing. I could lock a guy up at eight o'clock tonight and when he got out tomorrow at noon, he'd get a conditional discharge. Guilty. Released on his own recognizance. "Don't do that again." Time served.

I don't want regular people fucked with. And if it's the last fucking voice in the wilderness crying "Stop!", then I'm going to be the guy. But nobody—no voice, no uproar—is going to come and say, "You did a good job, Gene. You did a good job, Brian. We're not going to fine you, we're not going to take away your vacation."

They just don't consider it a crime anymore to sit there and suck a jug of wine, understand?

So what am I doing? I'm batting my fucking head against the wall. . . .

If the New York City Police Department today was doing the job correctly—and I mean correctly according to the way the administration wants it done—you could not walk the streets in New York City. Decent, regular people could not walk the streets.

You say there's nothing wrong with guys sitting in doorways around Times Square, right? There's no violation of the law, right?

OK. The Supreme Court says that the loitering law will be knocked down because it's been used indiscriminately by police officers to harass minority groups.

Who the hell is doing the loitering out there? Do you see sixteen guys in seersucker suits and attaché cases hanging out on corners and sucking jugs?

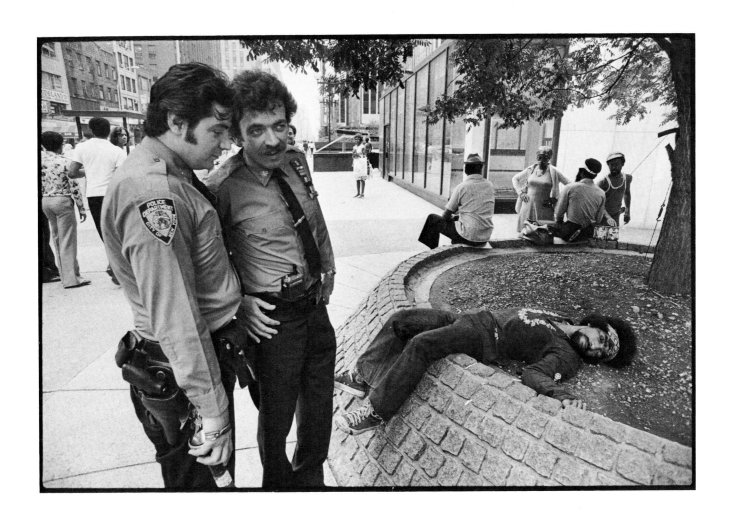

There's this wino standing on the corner of Eighth Avenue and 30th Street. A police officer tells him to move on and the guy turns around and throws a bottle at him, OK? So the cop goes over to talk to him and the guy whips out a fourteen-inch knife and stabs him in the chest. So the cop shoots him and kills him.

Okay, people say, "Winos don't bother anybody"—but where's the line going to be drawn?

Suppose just some regular guy is walking down the street. He's not a cop and he doesn't have a gun to protect himself. And somehow he gets involved with this mutt.

Now if this guy is going to pull a knife on a policeman, what do you think he's going to do to Joe Citizen?

We get a call to go to a movie theater on Broadway: "Man selling drugs in the lounge." They give a description:: "Black man, six feet . . ." The usual.

Gene and I go there, and here's this guy at the far end of the lounge—rolling joints.

"Gene, I just don't believe this. He's sitting there, right out in the open—and he's rolling joints."

We start walking toward him, and when he sees us, it's like the sky had opened up. *Baboom!*

"What are you doing?"

"Look, Officer, I'm just makin' some cigarettes."

"We can see that—but you're not supposed to be making up *those* type of cigarettes."

"No, no—this ain't grass, Officer. This is *possum flakes.*"

"What did you say?"

"Possum flakes. This ain't no grass, man."

"What do you mean, 'possum flakes'?"

"Just what I said, man—possum flakes."

So he tells us he bought a box of the stuff in a grocery store, then came up to the theater, dumped the contents in a brown-paper bag, and threw the container away in the garbage.

We go over and look in the garbage. And what do we find?

PARSLEY FLAKES.

You can't measure certain things, certain emotions. You can't measure fear. Like suppose your mother is driving home from the theater and she stops at Eighth Avenue and 45th Street and one of these winos comes over and starts washing the windshield.

She keeps the windows rolled up because she's afraid. OK? Now the guy says, "Give me a dollar for washing your window." It's not no quarter, either. "Give me a dollar for washing that window!" She refuses, but she's stuck in traffic. He starts pounding on the window. Cursing, yelling: "Open the window, you motherfucker! Give me some money!" OK?

What has he done? He's instilled fear in people. Now, a policeman goes by, sees that, and grabs the guy and takes him away. What do you lock him up for? Washing windows?

That's fear, and that's the fear I don't want any person to feel—bourgeois, Joe Turkey, anybody. I don't want them to feel it. And if anybody thinks that's penny ante, I think the guy's got his head up his ass.

Now when some guy demands money from you and you give him money because you're frightened, that's robbery. Robbery is a felony in New York. "Give me the money!" So why do you give him the money? Because you're afraid. That is a felony. That isn't some chicken-ass, penny-ante shit that the police shouldn't be involved in. OK?

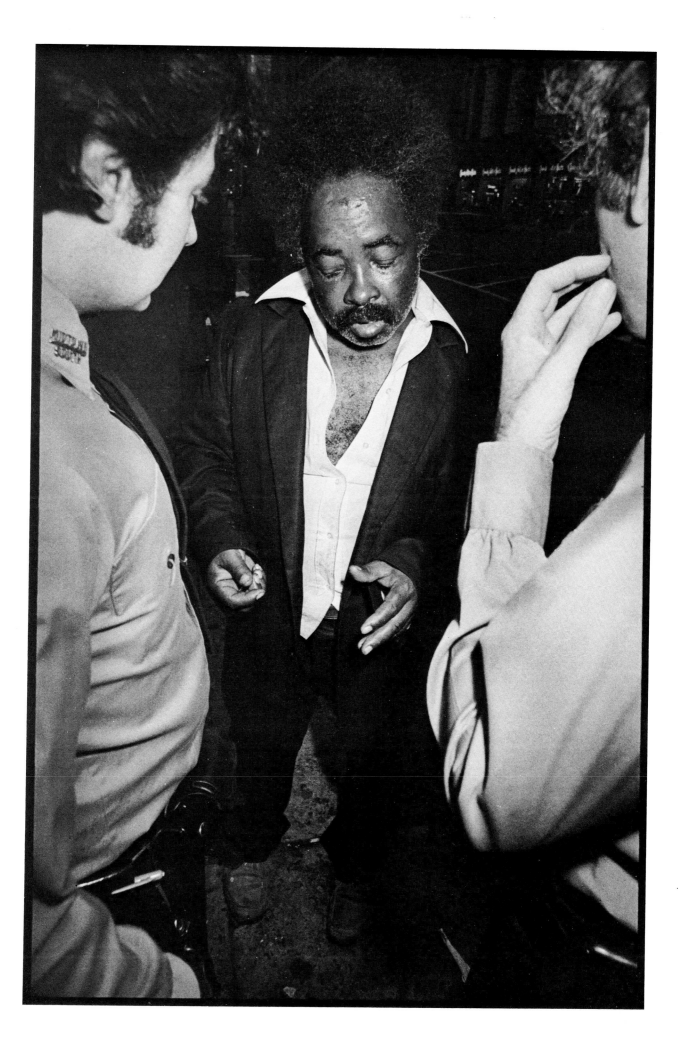

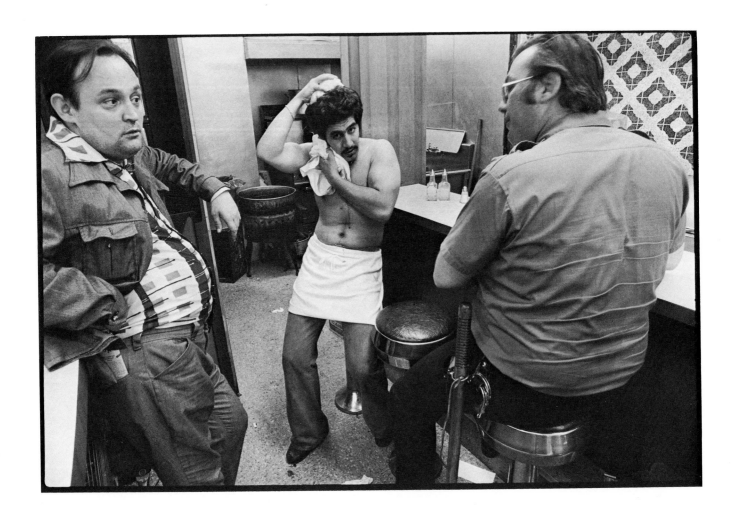

Suppose Michelangelo had to spend most of his time dealing with robbers and street bandits. How many statues, how many works of art would never have been created?

I don't think it's fair to ask people to be productive members of society while they still have to contend with people who would rip them off—just because they have something that the rippers don't.

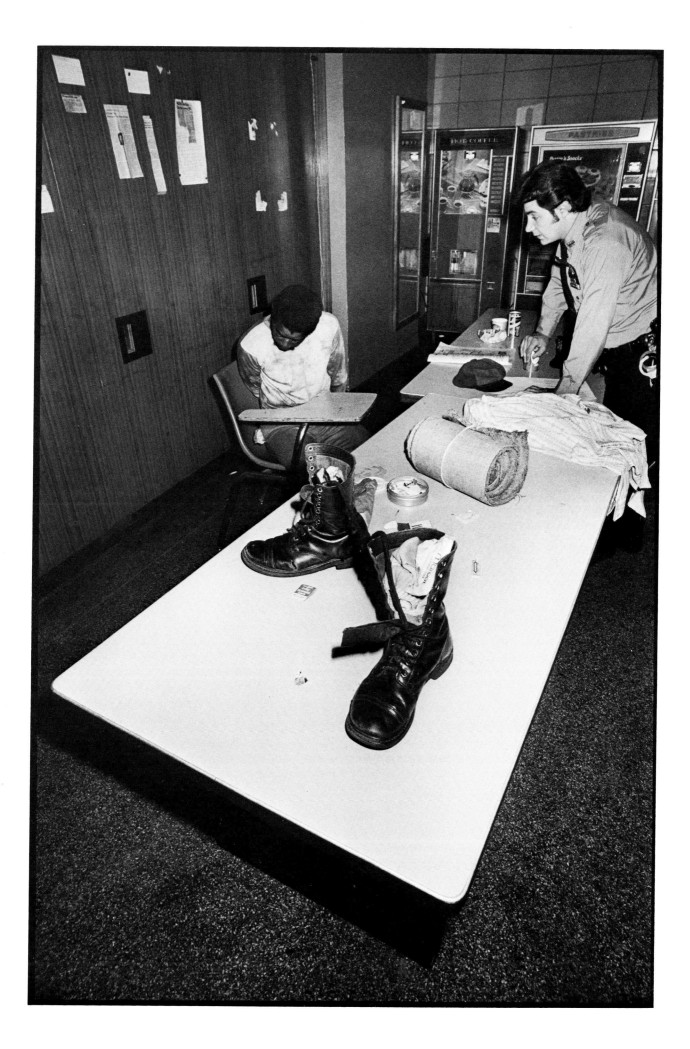

The average wino, the kind we have to deal with, is not the guy who's had too much to drink at a cocktail party. He's not the guy who sits in a bar getting loaded while he's watching a baseball game. He's a bum who makes his whole life out of living on the street and living off other people.

And there are a lot of them around. Like the one we picked up in front of the public library. Somebody had called 911 to report "a man down at 41st and Fifth."

We answered the call and got there at just about the same time as the ambulance. And what did we find? A drunk, lying on the sidewalk. Normally, we would've just left him there, but since somebody had reported him, we had to do something.

So we put him in the ambulance, and what does he do? He messes up the whole inside—the sheets, everything. Now this guy was in no danger of being arrested. All he would be was "an aided case." But he didn't want to know about that, he didn't want any "aid" at all. All he wanted to do was give us a hard time.

Just then, the ambulance driver told us that he'd gotten an emergency call on his radio. Now we certainly weren't going to immobilize an ambulance just for one drunk. So we got him out of the ambulance and started walking him across town on 41st Street. We finally found a freight entrance to a building between Fifth and Madison. The elevator was on the ground floor, there wasn't anybody around—it was late on a Friday afternoon—and the motor that worked the elevator had been turned off for the weekend.

We put the drunk in the elevator, and then, court was in session: the Judge and the Prosecutor were both wearing blue uniforms.

"What's the charge?"

"Public intoxication."

"Has the defendant anything to say?"

Apparently he didn't.

"Guilty. The sentence is three days. Case closed."

Bang!

It wasn't the Judge's gavel—only the elevator gates.

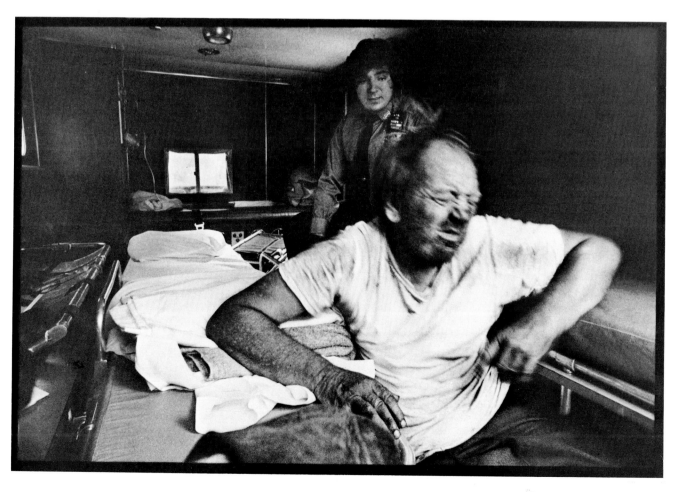

Better precincts? Fancier uniforms? I don't want any of that. Most cops don't want any of that.

The only thing I want is for people to go down the street and say, "There's the police and I don't have any fear." Anybody—black, white—anybody that's decent, that's law-abiding. That sounds like rhetoric from right-wing organizations—"decent," "law-abiding"—but that's the only words I can use.

I'll go out there in fucking rags if that's what it takes to make people secure. But paying me more money isn't going to erase the fear that a sixty-five-year-old lady is going to feel walking down the street. More money and fancy uniforms don't mean shit.

It seems to me as though we're just keeping the lid on something. We're just out there to do that, to keep a lid on it. And you know all the time that somebody could take the pressure off the bottom, there is a way to do it.

But they won't do it. Politically, it's not advantageous for someone to stand up and say, "This shit has got to end, and I'm going to put an end to it." When was the last time you heard a mayor get up and say, "I'm putting all people on notice that I'm not tolerating crime in this city. We just won't tolerate it. Whatever we have to do to make you realize that we don't want it, that's what we'll do"?

Nobody really cares. Sure, they talk about it, but do you think the mayor really gives a shit about people walking down the street and getting mugged? I doubt it very much.

Suppose this guy is in the Mafia. All right? He's Italian. He's a fucking criminal. I don't say, "Well, the guy is Italian. He's a bad guy." He's a guinea, motherfucking bastard. He deserves to go to jail. Right?

I don't make any excuses for him. I'm not going to tell you, "He was misunderstood, he was the victim of an early childhood; he was deprived—he only had one mother and one father; the phone only rang when somebody was calling." You know, all the outlandish excuses, all the bullshit rhetoric we've been handed for twenty years. And people nod their heads and say, "Yes, you're right, you're right. . . ."

Wrong! You play the game, you lose. That's it.

Certain organizations, the NAACP or the ACLU, say that when a guy commits a crime and he's black, he's a misunderstood youth.

That's no good. The guy's a criminal, he's black, and he should go to jail. That's all there is to it.

The president of the Guardians claims that black cops are black men before they're police officers and that they've got to keep their ethnic pride.

What ethnic pride do I have? I have a blue suit—that's the only thing I'm proud of.

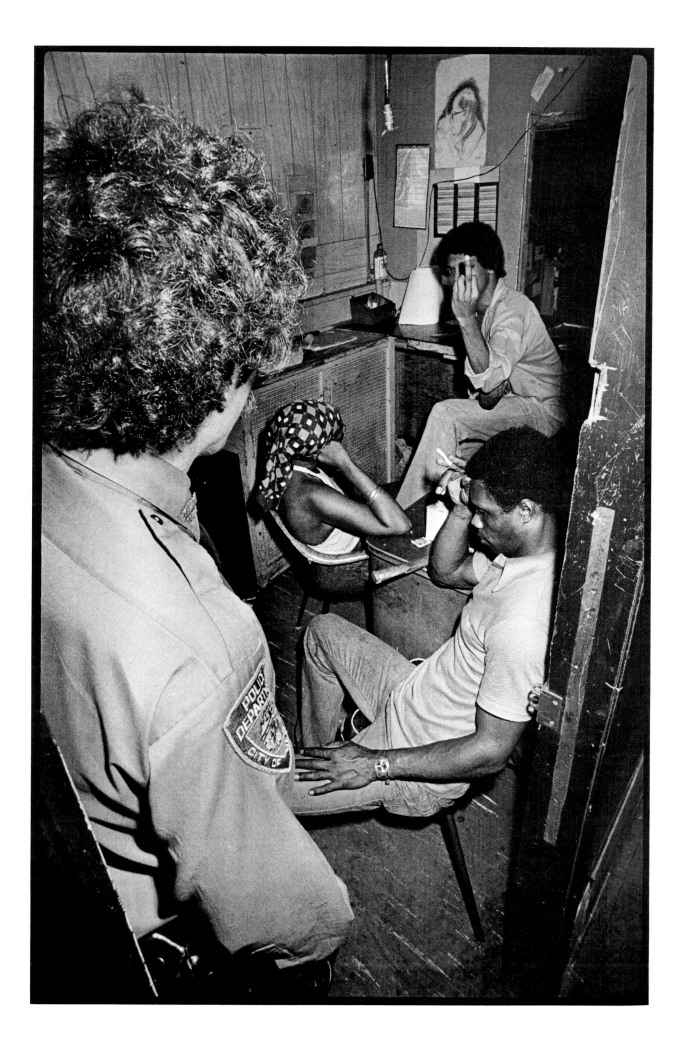

The Guardians is the black association inside the Police Department like the Emerald Society for the Irish and the Columbians for the Italians. The Emerald Society and the Columbians are fraternal organizations to promote brotherhood and parties and bullshit like that. The Guardians is a racial organization that promotes hatred. They work hand in hand with the NAACP and CORE and all the other shit. They work so that the nigger can be on top and the white guy can be on the bottom. They say that they're black men before they're police officers.

I don't think of that. When I catch a guy—he can be Irish, he can be Italian, he can be anything—I say, "He's a perp." He's nothing else. But the Guardians would say, "He's black."

Nobody makes any claim to being a white man first and a cop second. But the Guardians say in public that they're black men first. And nobody has the balls to take away their shields.

Your appearance on the street is very important to this job, especially for a quasi-military organization like we got here. We deal a lot with the public, and you know the public—their opinions are based on appearances. That's the name of the game—like the making of the President.

Now if I think a guy has long hair and it enhances his looks, fine. I'll go along with that. But if I see a guy with long hair and he looks like a gorilla, I mean, what the hell . . .

There's a guy here who has a beard, all right? I don't resent the beard as much as the tactics he used to keep the beard. Here you got five hundred men—and here's a guy who goes to the doctor and claims he has a skin disease. Now you know as well as anybody that he's full of shit. Right? So he goes and gets this note, this piece of shit, saying that he can't shave.

Now I don't resent the beard. But why should he be a privileged character, to have that beard when five hundred guys go along with the law against beards? That's not fair.

I'm determined to get that beard off that guy. And I'm going to get it off that guy, not because he looks, you know, like a skel, but because of the bullshit he pulled. It's the principle of the thing.

(The bearded police officer described here was eventually transferred to a narcotics division; shortly after that, he was arrested for skimming some of the drugs he was "buying" to establish evidence. Since then, he has reportedly "quit the job"—and gone to work for the Board of Education.)

About three o'clock one afternoon, we got a run that there was a guy in a building on Seventh Avenue holding some people hostage on the 18th floor. So we went upstairs and the first thing we see in this office is a little window where the secretary stands. She told us there was a guy in there holding everybody with a gun.

There was a door over on the side. I tried to get through it, but it was locked. So my partner Chip took his gun out, climbed through the little window, and told the guy inside to drop his gun. The guy turned around and pointed his gun in Chip's direction.

"If you come in here, I'm going to kill you, and I'm going to kill them."

"You better drop the fucking gun or I'll kill you," Chip told him.

So the guy dropped the gun, and we handcuffed him. He had some story about doing some contract work for this garment firm that they hadn't paid him for. So that day, he'd come up there with a gun and made them write out a check—for four or five thousand dollars more than they owed him.

Anyway, we took him in and the next day, he was in court. Now the complainants were scared stiff of this guy—they were afraid he was going to come back and shoot them. But the DA practically guaranteed them that this guy was going to jail and that there was no way he'd get out.

So the guy went before the judge—and the judge let him go. He said, "Make sure you don't go back to that place. Stay away from these people, or I'll put you in jail."

"They owe me money. I'm going back."

"Don't go back there!"

And as the guy was leaving the courtroom, he said, "I'm going back."

And that was the end.

Except for this. Earlier, when Chip was up for a promotion, he didn't get it. And why? Because in this job, they got lists. "Overweight List"—that's what's called the "Fat List"—"Chronic Sick List," stuff like that. There's a list called "Red Flag," which they use for cops they consider too aggressive. Another one is called "Rebel Cop," which means you're a loudmouth or a boss fighter. And once you're on one, you don't get off it—they bury you with it.

So why didn't Chip get promoted? Because he was on the "Fat List"—and this is the same guy that got through that little window to where the hostages were being held, right?

One day we were called to a tennis club on West 31st Street; some people there were complaining of BBs being fired at them while they played tennis. They said some of the BBs had penetrated the canvas covering the courts.

I don't know if anyone has ever been killed by a BB gun, but I'm sure being hit by one would be extremely painful. At the very least.

Anyway, it was obvious that the shots were coming from a welfare hotel across the street. However, there was little we could do about it—no one had actually seen anyone doing anything. Could we search the upper floors of the hotel? Maybe even by force? Legally?

No way!

All we could say to these people was "Sorry, there's nothing more we can do but file a report." They thanked us politely for coming, but they were clearly *not* impressed by the police service.

These things are frustrating when you're eager to help people but you can't. And they're going to go on until someone gets hurt.

One of the officers in our Precinct sees this girl commit a traffic violation, and when he tells her to pull over, she makes an obscene gesture. She gives him the finger.

So he arrests the girl for harassment, brings her into the station house, does all the paper work, and then lets the girl make a phone call.

She calls her father, and he comes down. He's a big shot in the garment area. You know, well dressed, lots of money, the whole spiel. So he walks in and says, "Who's the cop that arrested my daughter?" The cop says, "Here I am," and he gives the father the whole story—the traffic violation, the obscene gesture.

So the father goes over and asks his daughter, "Did you do that?" And she says, "Yes, I did that." And the father hauls off and smacks her right in the mouth and lays her out.

My worst moment on the job was the night of the blackout in Flatbush. I was never more frightened because we were fighting an enemy we couldn't see. It was like being in Vietnam, worse than Vietnam. And I hope it never happens again.

People were running around with property, breaking into stores, and running out fast—and the police could do nothing about it.

They had absolutely no regard for the police at all. The police weren't using their firearms to stop them, and they were being fired upon by snipers from buildings and bottles were being thrown.

They were setting fires to buildings, in their own neighborhoods, where women and children and probably their own relatives lived.

One day, my daughter is in school and the teacher comes up with this question: "What is the most difficult thing for you to go home and say to your father?" And he lists six or seven different things.

The kids are sitting there, thinking, and my daughter throws up her hand.

"You have an answer?"

"Yes, but it's not one of the things you have listed up there."

"What's the answer?"

"The hardest thing in the world for me to do is to tell my father that I'm engaged to a black man."

"Why?"

"Because my father is a cop in Times Square."

It was a real hot July day—125 degrees—and there were these four people—a man, his wife, and their two kids—who had come down from upstate New York just to see the All-Star Game. They had gone into a coffee shop on Broadway, and while they were in there, somebody stole the woman's purse from the back of her chair. Not only that, the guy that did it took the key to their hotel room out of the purse, went there, and stole their binoculars.

By the time we learned about it, there wasn't much to be done. But we did do this—we put in a call to the precinct near Yankee Stadium and then we sent the family up there to see them. That was all we could do.

About a month later, we learned the rest of the story. And it's this kind of thing that makes our job worth doing.

Edda I.
Wurtsboro, N.Y. 12790
August 15, 1977

Dear Mr. McMenamin,

I'm sorry I couldn't write this letter earlier. I want to thank you very much for all you did to help us get into the All-Star Game in July. The police at Yankee Stadium referred us to the proper authorities and we saw the game. The kids were very happy.

And you wouldn't believe what happened to my stolen pocketbook. The thief came back to the hotel in the early morning and hung the pocketbook on my hotel room door. The money, the bus tickets, plus the tickets to the All-Star Game were taken, but my house keys and my car keys plus important papers were returned.

I want to thank you very much. The New York City Police are great and much appreciated.

Thanks again,
Edda I. and kids
from Wurtsboro

It seems blacks handle violence better than whites. Because they're used to it. They grew up with it.

Madison Avenue and 38th Street.

In a card shop, the owner, a sixty-four-year-old white male, is shot in the face. His customer, an eighty-two-year-old black female, is shot in the chest by two black guys wearing ski masks.

Policemen are called on emergency to the premises. Our patrol car opened the road to the Emergency House for two ambulances.

The sixty-four-year-old man is brought directly to the emergency block, barely conscious. He is emotionally choked, which increases the gravity of his case.

As for Lucille Clarke, the eighty-two-year-old lady who was shot in the chest during the stickup, she thought she had a heart attack. When she found out she had a bullet wound, she didn't want to go to the hospital.

In the emergency room, when she saw the intern pointing a needle at her arm, she waved her hands, saying, "No, no, no! I don't need a shot. I'm all right!"

She kept her handbag held tightly against her, the handbag she grabbed away from the policeman escorting her—and spent some time on the phone with an old friend telling her all about what happened. We were amazed at her faculty of recuperation. We had a long talk with her; this was her statement:

"I was in the store next door. I wanted to get something for my brother for Father's Day because I didn't get anything yet. I walked into the card shop and got hit. I heard more shots, so I got down on my knees in the corner to pray."

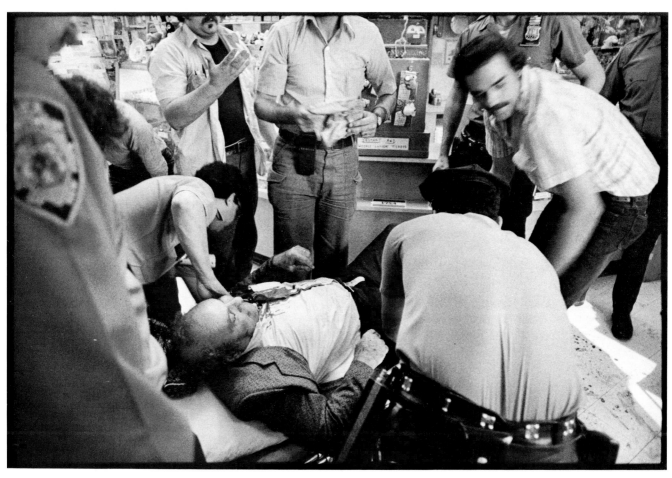

This guy Calvin Jones was supposed to get the electric chair. In '63, he had killed a police officer. In this Precinct. He was tried and convicted. Capital punishment, okay?

But Rockefeller commuted his sentence. And after that, the guy showed up every day in prison, he woke up, he ate his food, he didn't cause any trouble.

So he did seven years and was released—he's out now. He's out there right now on Times Square. He's a bag hustler, a thief, and a stickup man. And he was arrested a month ago for armed robbery in Grand Central Station. Calvin Jones.

Pornography is the first thing everybody points to in Times Square. But the people you see in Times Square, hanging around, aren't there for the porno movies. The guys going into the porno movies are the guys with the attaché cases and the seersucker suits.

Then you have the mutts in the street. They don't go to porno movies. They're either looking to deal drugs or rip people off, and they have no correlation with the sex trade there.

Of course, there are plenty of people that do make their living off the sex trade. Not only people running porno movies, but weirdo shops and stuff like that. Like the guy from the peep show that Jaydie took a picture of. The guy gets real angry and comes over and says, "You! I saw you take that picture. I'm taking out a contract on you right now—and tomorrow, you're gonna be dead."

Maybe pornography has something to do with prostitution. Maybe the prostitutes can work a guy over after he comes out of one of these shows, the guy who comes in from Minneapolis or from Jersey. Everyone comes over from Jersey to get laid.

Rain is the best policeman in the world. It serves to keep people off the street.

We're coming down Broadway once, me and Brian, and we make a turn on 45th Street. As we turn, there's this guy standing there, a black guy, and he runs away. We aren't after him, but when we get back to Broadway, we look around to see where he's gone. You know, just casually.

There's this other dude standing there, laughing, and he says, "I don't know, Officer. He went right down *into the earff*!"

Oh, *the earff*, huh. And that was it. Then we just drove away.

Earff!

You really had to be there. . . .

When Audrey sees our squad car, she always stops to talk with Gene.

"Where are you from, Audrey?"

"I am from Pennsylvania. I grew up in Hollywood. Those days, they never went after girls who weren't under thirty. . . . Clark Gable was the only sexy one. . . ."

"How about W. C. Fields?"

"Like any alcoholic. . . . Rock Hudson did not show the usual form of his homosexuality. . . . Marlon Brando, Elvis Presley, they got in trouble with the cops because of their motorcycles. . . .

"The worst woman was Zsa Zsa Gabor—the more beautiful they are, the more skinkessaud they get."

"Where are you living now, Audrey?"

"Same place, they busted my door. . . . They trying to play the same trick on me. You can't find a place over there—the prices are up."

"Why you staying there?"

"You can take a bath—it's nice, like in any good whorehouse. . . .

"Any time I get a steady boyfriend I let him go. I was married once—somehow it never worked."

"What about girlfriends?"

"I can't stand the other girls."

"Are you on welfare now?"

"It's all part of the same old crusade. I tried to work in a drugstore. Just two weeks later the place was closed down. So what kind of job is that?"

"Did you steal anything during the blackout, Audrey?"

"I ain't gonna rob a store just to be robbed again by my neighbors."

One night, in front of the Midtown South Precinct, we were waiting for a squad car with Brian, when a man with blond curly hair, a mustache, and tattoos all over his arms walks up to Brian and asks him, "Are you a policeman?"

Brian is in uniform. "Yes?"

"I just swallowed two razor blades."

"Go make a report in the police station."

The man goes up the stairs, opens the first double doors, sees Gene, and tells him, "I just swallowed two razor blades!"

"Why don't you go to a hospital?"

"O-Okay . . ." And the man opens the second set of doors and bangs his head so hard that he falls to his knees. He is bleeding all over the place. The switchboard officer calls for an ambulance. But when it gets there, the guy refuses any medical attention.

"This guy's a psycho! If I had two Band-Aids, I would've fed them to him."

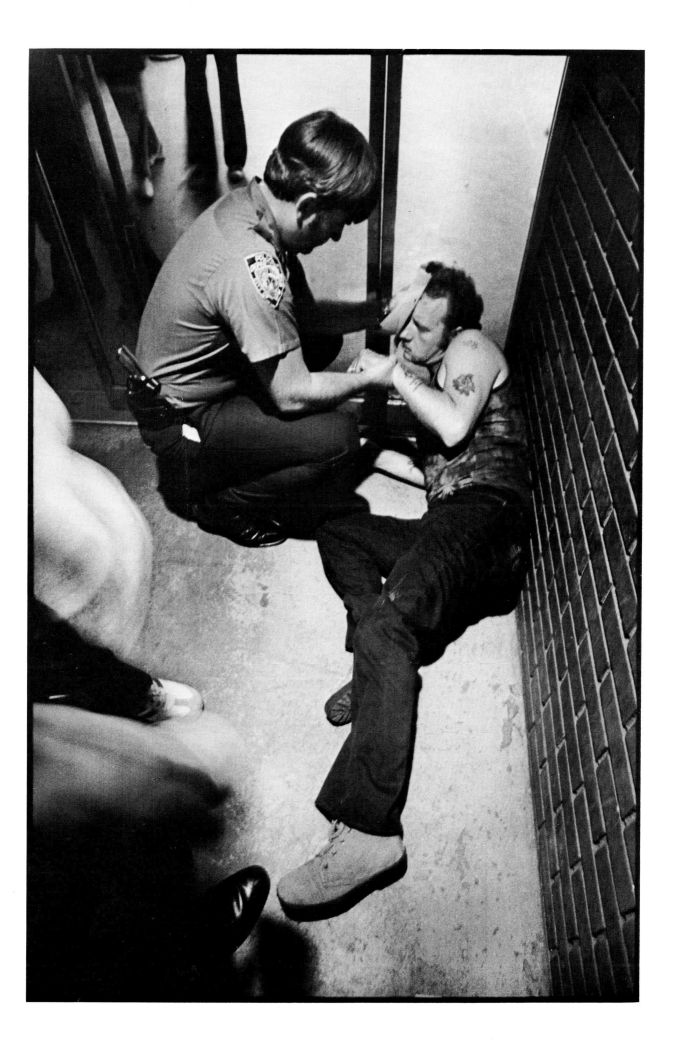

I like psychos. Psychos are great. Psychos make me think of myself as a lion tamer. A lion tamer goes in all by himself with all those lions around him. Any one of them could do him in in a minute. But somehow, by being around them enough, by learning their habits, he's got them under control.

And the more you talk with psychos, the more you deal with them, the more you see how they react to certain things. Each day, you build a block. In this job, you're building a wall. And each day, you try to learn something, you try to get it right. Each day you talk to them you learn a different way to handle them.

At any moment, one of those psychos in the Times Square area could become violent. I've seen harmless psychos go violent. Like this one psycho that was a buff besides. And he was a very nice guy. But one day, he went berserk and he fucked up two cops. And a little while after that, he jumped in front of a subway train trying to kill himself. The only thing he managed to do was cut off all his fingers and most of both hands. Now he's in a VA hospital where he'll probably stay until he dies.

Sylvia's a psycho. She's been in the Precinct for years. She hasn't changed much, only now she walks with a couple of canes. I don't know why. She's not a violent psycho, she's a friendly psycho. She wears a tremendous amount of makeup.

There's another one who wears even more makeup than her. I guess she's on welfare or something like that. I've seen her with men. It's not like she's not going out with guys. Maybe she's turning tricks with guys. Who knows? Basically, she's just a person I see on 44th Street all the time.

Most psychos you find are dropouts from society—besides everything else. They don't want their parents or their children to know where they are. Like the one we met last night is a psycho we've known for a long time. From the Sloane House. She comes over and tells us she gets raped there once a week. Imagination, basically. Maybe she gets robbed, maybe. . . . There's no question about that. Last night, what was she complaining about? Someone took her bag—the FBI, all that sort of bullshit. She's a psycho. We have hundreds of them in the city. Right here in midtown. What are you going to do?

In all other jobs, a guy can sit down or go take a piss without someone breathing down his neck. But here, they break your balls—if they want to break your balls.

One day, me and Brian are in G and G when Pat, who's this big Irish guy, walks in and says, "Hey, Officer, there's a guy just parked his car down the block, and he's coming this way. He looks like an inspector or something."

This guy has an oak leaf, he's a deputy inspector. That's his job. To go out and catch cops. That's what he thinks his job is. A shoofly. He grabs us coming out the door. "What's going on here? What are you men doing?"

"There was a little trouble in here, Inspector. We straightened it out."

"Oh, really??"

So he goes in and grabs Gus. "What were those cops doing here?"

The balls of this guy—not to believe us!

Gus says, "There was some trouble in here"—he hadn't even heard us—"and these two officers came by and straightened it out."

"Oh. Okay."

Now the guy's fucked because he sees that we were doing the right thing. But now, he's got to find something. "Let me see your memo books."

So he looks at my memo book, which is three days behind. He doesn't even realize it. And Brian's book is like five days behind. And the inspector signs it—on Brian's day off. That's how fucked up this guy is. Finally, he tells us, "You know you're supposed to have all your entries, you're supposed to know how much oil is in your car. . . ." Plus all the other chicken-ass, Mickey Mouse shit.

Okay. We get in the car and leave.

Shooflies . . .

Dominic and Tony are in the back of G and G one night when this guy Pat walks in. He's got his hands all cut up, and he's yelling and cursing.

"I should've broken that motherfucker's ass!" All that kind of thing.

Now at the time, *American Buffalo* was playing in the theater right next door, so there's a lot of regular people in there. And here's this guy with his hands cut up, yelling all this stuff.

Then Pat goes in the back and picks up a six-pack of beer. Dominic and Tony are standing there talking, and Pat sees them and says, "Oh, you fucking cops! If you didn't have a gun, I'd break your fucking ass!"

They laugh and say, "Go on, Pat. Go home."

So he's got this six-pack under his arm, and as he goes out, he says to one of the brothers that owns the place, "Put it on my bill."

"Wait a minute. You don't have a bill here."

So now Dominic says to Pat, "Hey! Come back with that beer!"

Pat turns around and throws the six-pack at Tony. Almost hits him. Tony goes to grab him, and he rips Tony's jacket right off him. Pat's real strong, and he's fighting them, and they're trying to calm him down.

By now, there's a whole group of people around, and they're yelling, "Hey! Stop that! Leave that old man alone!" They think the cops are mugging him.

"That old man" is only about fifty, and he's fighting like an animal.

One of the owners of the French restaurant next door comes over and says, "Look, those cops are only trying to lock the guy up. Mind your own business!"

"Police brutality! Police brutality!"

Meanwhile, one of the brothers has called the police, and two radio cars show up. Pat is going berserk, fighting and kicking, banging his head against the wall. Completely snapped.

They get him back to the Precinct and lock him up. And he's standing there yelling, "All my black brothers! All my Puerto Rican brothers! Help me!" Which is ridiculous because he hates those guys—he's always out in the street fighting with them.

He goes to court, they make him pay for the cop's jacket, they psycho him out, and send him to Bellevue.

Three days later, he's out on medication. He sees me in the car and says, "I'm taking these pills, and I can't come down. I know I was wrong that night. I've got to kill myself. Can you lend me your gun? I'm going to blow my head off."

The string is snapped. He's gone.

"What am I going to tell you, Pat? Go home and relax."

Now here's a guy who isn't some raving lunatic, who's usually clean and well-dressed. A decent psycho.

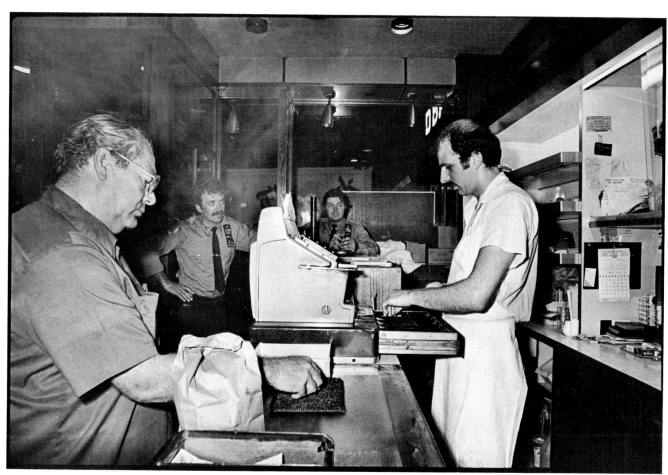

One night, this cop named Richie was outside putting gas in his van when a guy came running out of the dark and started whacking Richie on the head with a claw hammer. He knocked him down and beat him all over the face and body.

There was an AP—an auxiliary—upstairs who saw what was going on and started yelling. So the guy ran off down 36th Street, leaving Richie laying there with his collarbone broken, his head fractured, and all these giant indentations in his face. Beat up real bad.

Some other cops took off after the guy, caught him, and brought him back. The guy was a psycho from Pennsylvania; he'd come here to get a gun, and he figured the best way to get one was to knock a cop off. Now there's a hardware store over on Eighth Avenue, and the guy went there to buy a hatchet, but he didn't have enough money for a hatchet, so he bought a claw hammer. And he used it on Richie.

So Richie's got a metal plate in his head.

And the guy got psychoed. He got nothing.

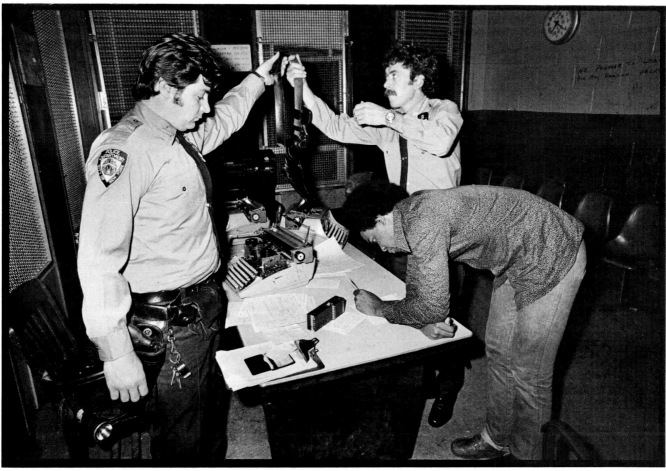

A lot of suicides happen in hotels. They usually find them on the day tours. When the maids go and unlock the doors. They die at night. Because at night, they're all alone.

People commit suicide a lot around the holiday season. Because they don't have any family. Or because they think they don't have anybody who wants them.

There's this hotel in the Times Square area that used to be a good hotel. People still go there, of course, maybe people on a tour from out of state. I mean, you still see buses lined up there. Because it's in the heart of New York City.

On a couple of floors, they've got people on methadone maintenance programs. Those are the mutts that are on drugs but not heroin anymore. They give them methadone so they can curb their appetite for heroin. They're scumbags. Another floor has outpatients from Bellevue Hospital who are psychos. They don't have any more room for them in Bellevue—or they say they don't have any more room—so they put them there. Another floor has convicted people from prison on work-relief programs. They stay there while they go to work, wherever the fuck they go to work.

So it's like a halfway house for cons, drug addicts, and psychos. The entire hotel is riddled with shit. People come in from Asshole, Kentucky, and they get ripped off. And they get hurt. A lot of times.

I remember these people from Canada. They'd won some contest: "Two Glorious Weeks in Midtown New York." And they wound up in that hotel.

We met them in Mike's place, and I told them about the hotel. And they said, "We can't believe it's like that." So I told them again. And they said, "Oh, we'd better leave. But we just won this two-week vacation."

Well, what's it worth? Two weeks sitting there—and maybe not making it to the second week? Anyhow, I guess they packed up and left—they weren't too happy with the accommodation.

In a place like that, it's "Gimme the money, Honey!" Okay? The money's green because it's coming from New York State or from the federal government.

I know another hotel that was also a very nice hotel at one time. Now there's nothing in there but welfare shit. Nothing but.

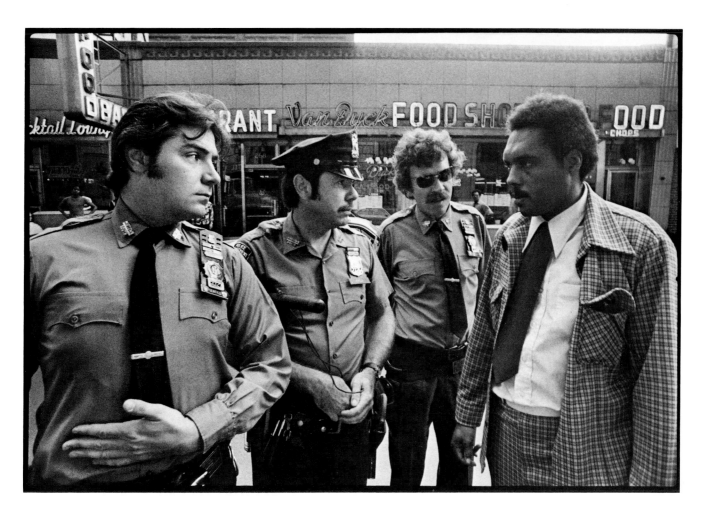

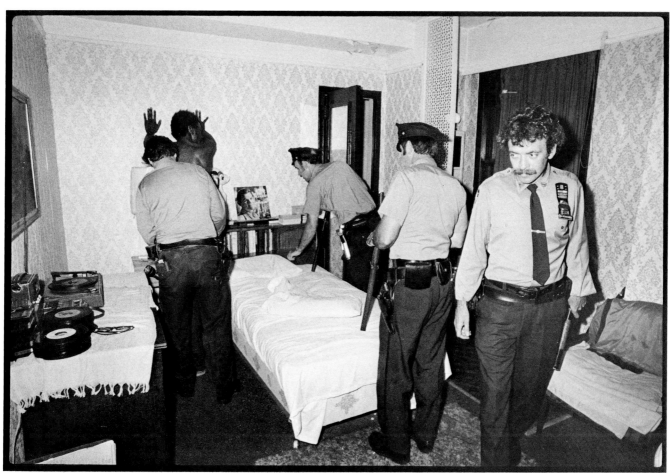

Take that guy, for example.

What's he doing? Nothing—he's just standing there, right?

But wait a minute! That guy's a karate master—and he can kill you with his feet, with his hands, or with those little metal balls he's got. So that's *three* deadly weapons he's in possession of. And what can we do about it?

Nothing . . .

Look! I don't like my picture taken.

I'm not in Russia. I'm in the United States, and I have a right to privacy, understand?

Why don't you go out and take pictures that are involved with this country—"indirectly" and "inadvertently" and "top secretwise"?

You got a beard. You got a long beard. You got a camera. Why don't you straighten out those cops?

I'm telling you I don't want you taking my picture. Can you dig it? I've been aggravated by this broad and now you're going to come here and aggravate me with your jive little camera. You're going to show off the fact you got an expensive camera. Is that what you're trying to do?

You got some bullshit white folks in this country who don't know what's happening. Like they don't even know what's happening. You know!

This is mine. This is my country. I was born here. You better watch what you're doing, man. This is my country. I love this country.

You better not photograph me.

Probably 90 percent of he/shes have man-made breasts—but still have outdoor plumbing. Maybe 10 percent get the whole job done.

There used to be a bus terminal over behind Woolworth's, and part of our regular procedure was going around to the lots in back and chasing the whores and their johns out of there.

So one night, we see a couple in this car. There's a little guy inside, and he's banging away like crazy. So we go up to the car.

"Hey!"

The guy gets out of the car and says, "What's the matter? I'm a working man—I ain't bothering nobody. . . ."

"But you're with a man," we tell him.

So now his eyes are like a slot machine. *Whirrr!*

"What?"

"You're with a man. . . ."

"Don't tell me I'm with a man!"

"That's what we're telling you. . . ."

Now, what these he/shes used to do was, they'd never pull their shorts all the way down, they'd just pull them on the side. So it would wind up that the guy was screwing them in the ass.

So we got the he/she out of the car. "Drop your laundry!"

He drops his laundry, and here's this big Johnson like this. An air hose. And the little guy—he's ready to kill!

One time, we pull up to a car in some lot. Inside, there's a guy sitting at the wheel, facing into the lot with his back to the street, holding on to the wheel. And is he holding on!

We bang on the window.

"Let's see your license and registration."

He's got this he/she in there with him, right? So he starts mumbling—in Greek.

"Come on—the paperwork!"

And he mumbles some more. So Brian says to him:

"You know what you got there, pal?" And he points to the he/she. "This is a *guy*, you understand? A guy!"

So the "Greek" that couldn't speak English says, "Hey! What about my ten dollars?"

Another time, there's this bunch of white guys, probably over from New Jersey, hanging out on Ninth Avenue. And they're playing their games with the he/shes. So we decide we'll do the right thing—we'll straighten them out.

We pull the car across the street and call one guy over.

"Look, we don't know what you guys are up to, but we just want to let you know that these are not women but men."

"Yeah," the guy says, "I know—but they give the best blowjobs!"

So Gene says, "Let's get out of here! I've had enough of this guy!" He just couldn't believe that the guy had said that.

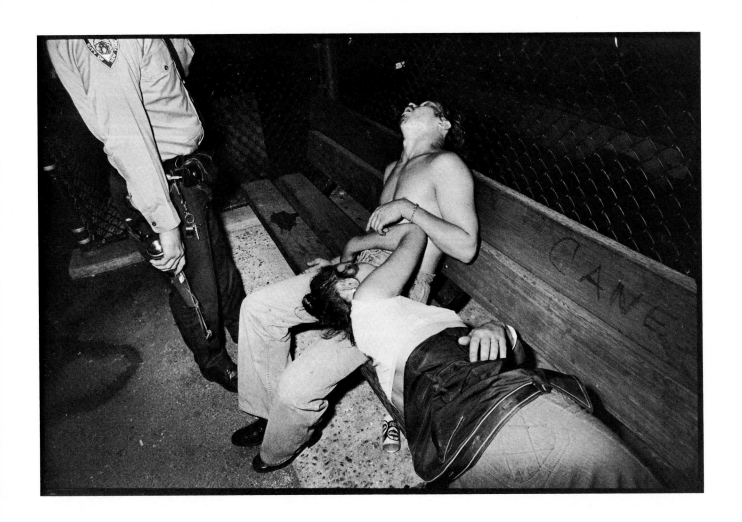

Every night, a couple of cops have to go and lock up this little park beside the Holy Cross Church on 42nd Street. Why? Because the priest got tired of finding bottles and rubbers and syringes there every morning. So now he comes regularly to the Precinct to make sure the captain is sending guys over to chase out the drunks and the whores and the junkies.

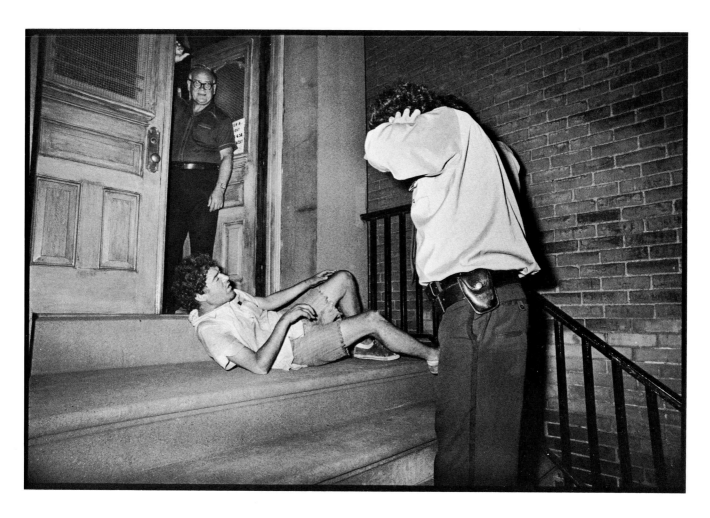

People have a lot of funny ideas about cops. They somehow think we just sit around in our cars or walk up and down our beat all day long. They imagine we never stop for lunch or a cup of coffee or anything.

I remember once I was coming out from taking a piss and a woman going in looked at me and said, "Oh—I never knew policemen went to the bathroom."

She really said that!

No matter how phony the call is, you have to go, and you have to investigate. No matter what.

One day, Kenny Cartwright and his partner got a call about two children that were abandoned outside Gimbels. One was nine years old, the other was four months old. Inside the carriage, they found some clothes that had obviously been shoplifted—there was no bag, no bill.

After about an hour, the mother—the so-called mother—came into the Precinct, kind of pissed off and embarrassed that the police knew what she was doing. And the first thing she did was to yell at the kids. But there was no arrest—it was just a call, and after that, Cartwright and his partner went back out to work.

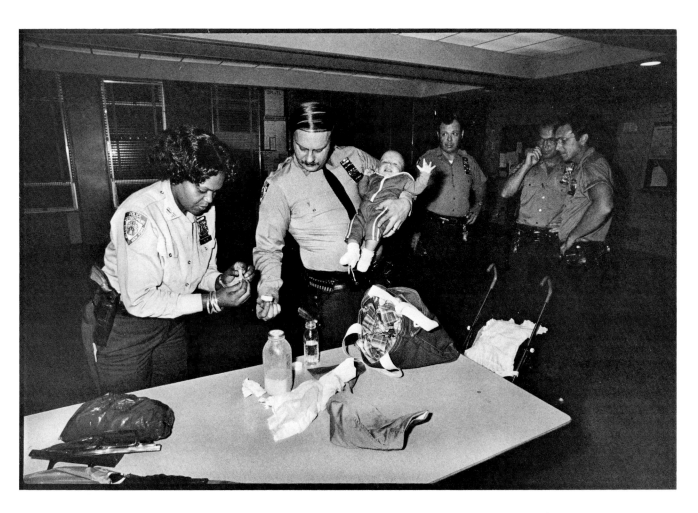

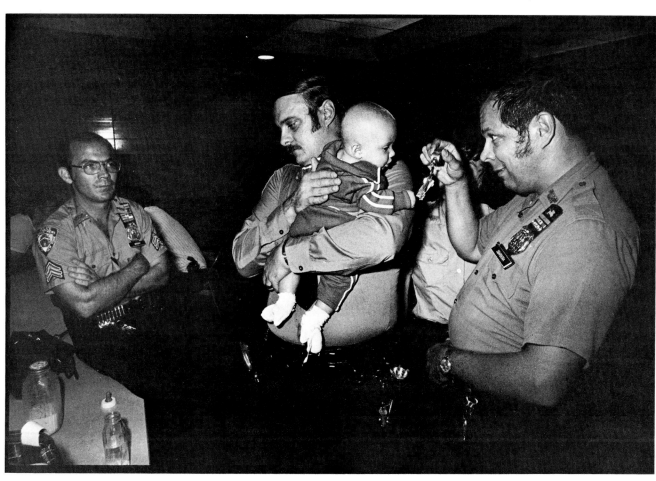

We got a call from the Long Island Rail Road police in Penn Station—they had a lost boy there, so they called "the precinct of record," which was us.

Now this was an Oriental kid, and on top of that, he was mentally retarded. He was fourteen, but he had the mentality of a kid six or seven. And coupled with the kid's mental problem was his Oriental accent, so it was extremely difficult to communicate with him.

Then it was phone calls all over the place—Missing Persons, Youth Aid Division. One cop we spoke to told us that he himself had a retarded kid, and that if we looked on the label of the kid's shirt or jacket, chances are we'd find his name, address, and telephone number. We looked, but all we could make out was the name. Well, we knew what train the LIRR police had gotten him from, and we started calling different precincts all over Nassau County.

Sure enough, we got a call back from a cop out there. Somebody was looking for that kid. And he said that not only was the kid retarded, but that he had this thing about going off on his own—he'd left his bike on the lawn, gotten on a train, and come to Manhattan. From Great Neck, Long Island!

Okay, so we had the name, address, and telephone number of the family. We called and got the kid's sister. She was about sixteen, and said her parents were frantic and had gone out looking for her brother. We gave her the name and address of the Precinct and said they could come and pick him up.

So it was all done, all over—and we went back out on patrol. And while we were gone, the mother came in. She had tears running down her cheeks—we'd found her boy, she wanted to thank us, she was so happy. . . .

And we were so elated. . . .

So when people ask what it's like to be a cop, all the chases, and the cowboys-and-Indians, all the other stuff—that isn't it. It's helping people—like when we got that kid back to his mother. It was one of the greatest experiences we ever had.

That's the reward.

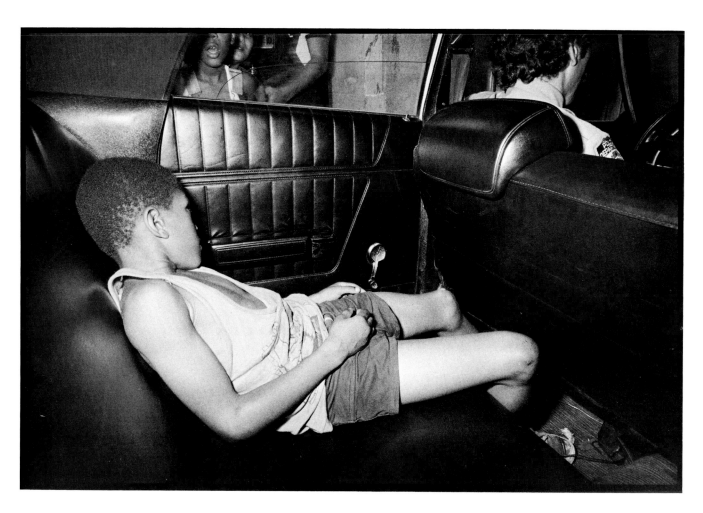

This guy Willie was something else. To begin with, he had a weird kind of job—he'd walk around Midtown and hand out flowers. And prospectuses for a massage parlor.

Okay, so one night he's doing this, and he sees a guy coming along 46th Street carrying a pound of grass. Willie gives him a flower, and the guy says, "Thank you."

Now Willie is standing there, looking at the guy's bag with the grass in it. "Why don't you lay a joint on me?"

"Why don't you try and take one off me?"

"I ain't gonna try. . . ."

"Go ahead."

Willie wants no part of this, so he starts to walk away. And that's when the guy takes out a knife, stabs him, and runs away.

So now Willie goes home; he takes off his shoes—if he wants to catch the guy, he's got to be able to run as fast as possible—he gets his knife, and he heads for The Apple—that's 42nd Street between Seventh and Eighth—because that's where he figures the guy will be.

On his way there, he's seen by one of the girls from the massage parlor. He's all bloody and messed up, so she tries to stop him. But Willie doesn't want to be stopped, and he pushes her away, knocking her down.

With this, the girl's boyfriend jumps into it, and Willie goes for him with his knife. And gets him—on the ear. But this wasn't even the guy Willie was after in the first place. . . .

When something like this happens in that area—a fight, a stabbing—people gather around very quickly, and before you know it, you've got a lot of trouble. That's why the first thing the police do is clear everybody away. And then they take a look at what's happened. . . .

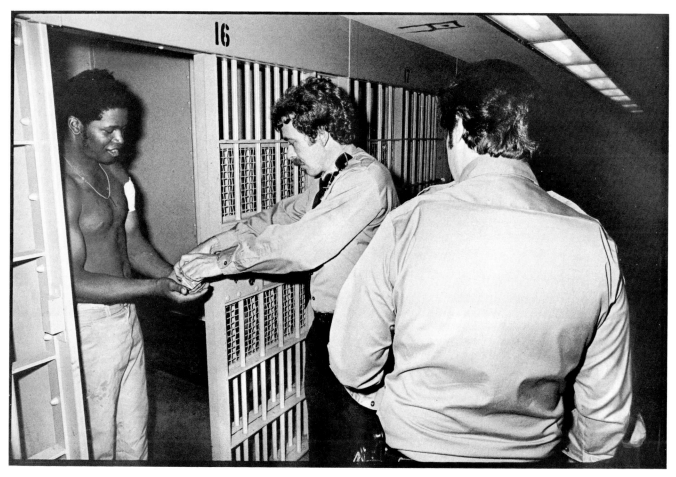

So there's a crowd all around this guy Willie who's got a knife in his hand and has just used it. On the other guy's ear. Gene first gets people to move out of the way, and then tries to get Willie and the other guy into a car and off to the hospital. No arrests—they'll just be "aided cases" and that'll be the end of it.

But when Willie sees Gene coming toward him, he resists. Which he shouldn't do. Gene finally gets a hold on him, and Willie calms down enough to say:

"Look, man, I was crazy! I mean, if I wasn't, I never would've—"

"Well, you can't be crazy now. You can be crazy all you want when the police aren't around, but when you see the blue uniform, you've got to stop."

"Hey! If somebody fucked with you, if somebody cut you, then—"

"Then fuck with him, don't fuck with the police."

All of a sudden, Willie gets real quiet.

"Y'all gonna shoot me now?"

"What? We aren't going to shoot you—because the last guy we shot bled all over the back of the car, and we had to clean it up!"

OK, it turned out later that Willie was from the Deep South, and down there, getting arrested is the same thing as getting shot. Or at least he'd always thought it was.

"Go ahead and kill me, man! I don't care!"

"You don't want to die—not with all those chicks out there, not when—"

"It ain't the chicks, man. . . ."

"—you could be getting high, having a good time. Why die now? You got a girlfriend?"

"Naw . . ."

"What about all the chicks in the massage parlor?"

"Hey, man—like I got a family back home I gotta support."

"Right. You're a working guy. So you shouldn't get involved in shit like this."

"But what if some guy cuts you, man?"

"That's terrible. Maybe you'll both go to jail. And when you get in the cell, you can straighten it out together. No knives. Fair enough?"

On the way to the hospital, Willie said, "I been in a foster home since I was ten years old. And I been beaten with everything from farm tools to bricks. . . ."

Now if that's true, it's unfortunate. But the very fact he said it ought to be an incentive for him. He's a big guy, so he could do something else—maybe loading trucks, anything—instead of working for a massage parlor. He's twenty-three years old, and if he can recognize that his life has been fucked up, he can change it.

But it isn't very likely he will.

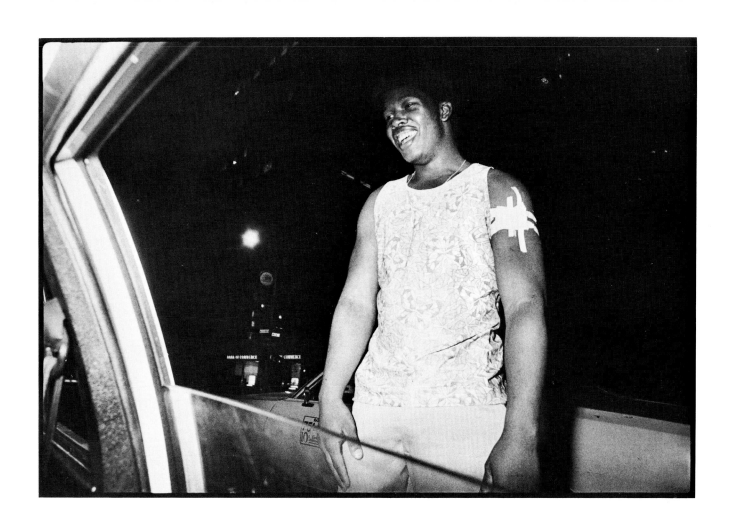

The first time it comes over, it's something like this: *"Man without any clothes on, 30th Street and Broadway. Check and advise."*

When we get to 30th and Broadway, he's gone. So then: *"We now have it as 30th and Fifth."* Thanks a lot.

We start heading east. And then it's 30th and Park. Okay—30th and Park. Finally, at 30th and Lex, we see two traffic men and they got this guy standing between two cars, balls-ass naked. And there's all these women hanging around, ogling his plumbing.

"Oh, mercy!"

Now understand, this guy is hung like a fucking donkey, he's got a schwanz and a half. And he's completely nonplussed, he couldn't care less.

And there's three chicks standing at a window. They got the curtains open and they're peering down into the street. So I point up at them—"What are you looking at?" And they jump back and turn out the lights.

When they got this man, he was already in the 13th Precinct, so those guys responded. They put a blanket around him, put him in a car, and then asked him why he did it.

"I was hot."

Hot? Now that really makes sense. The guy was really screwed up. Some kind of psycho.

Now psychos don't get busted, they're not an arrest. They're an "aided case."

They'll take a guy like that to the hospital and give him an examination. And maybe they'll release him in a couple of hours. And maybe he'll come home and jump in front of a train or something.

A cab driver is pulled over by a policeman on a horse. While the officer is writing out a ticket, the driver goes over and whispers something to the horse.

"Hey! What did you just say to my horse? My horse just got a hard-on."

"None of your business. You're going to give me a ticket, so there's no way I'll tell you."

Finally, the cop says, "Look, I'll tear up the ticket if you'll tell me what you said to the horse."

"I told the horse you're a cocksucker."

It was close to midnight, the end of our tour. We were on our way to the station house when we saw a young woman running after a man, like if her life depended on it. We realized that the guy was holding a handbag. "A purse snatcher!"

We started after him with the lights on and everything. Gene dodged his way through traffic to get to the west side of Sixth Avenue. In an effort to escape, the man turned down 45th Street. Gene ran the car up on the sidewalk right on the guy's heels. The mutt dropped the handbag, turned around, and raised up his hands. The car stopped short, an inch from him. The doors swung open. Gene and Brian jumped out so fast that in no time they were on the guy. They threw him up against the wall, and he assumed the position. Gene searched him for weapons and back-cuffed him.

The woman caught up with us. She was a young Korean who had just finished working in a restaurant and was walking home. All her LIFE was in that bag; money, identification, green card. She was so scared she couldn't stop shaking. She seemed even more frightened by the policemen than she was by the whole situation. I explained to her, with my foreign accent, that she had nothing to worry about. These officers were here to protect her. All they needed was a deposition. All she wanted was to go home (later she got a ride home).

She started to calm down.

In the meantime Gene discovered that the guy was carrying release and rehabilitation papers from prison and drug centers. "Why did you steal the bag?"

"To get some money for a fix."

"You're a dirtbag! You still taking shit?"

"Yes."

"Look what you're doing! Look how you've scared that girl! You're no good for society! All you are is trouble!"

"Yes, but I can't help myself! I'd kill myself if I could!"

"Why don't you do yourself a favor and jump off a fucking building?"

One night, at 260 West 41st Street, the victim, a black man, was seen arguing about money with a shorter man. A few minutes later, at 11:10, a call came through about a stabbing.

Ronald Williams Collins was lying with his face glued to the sidewalk, a knife in his back.

Police officer Mike Grasso bent over Collins's body. "Take it easy, man! You're going to be all right. Don't move. Now, listen to me, the ambulance's on its way. Can you talk? Tell me, who did it to you?"

Collins's face was twisted in pain, his eyes reflected a mixture of panic and anger. But when he talked, his voice was determined. "The guy Harvey did it."

"What does he look like?" asked Officer Grasso.

"Never you mind his looks," said Collins. "I's gone get him myself."

These two Transit Authority cops were having lunch one day when this Oriental man walked in and said there was a black guy trying to break into his car. The Transit cops stopped eating, went across the street, and approached the guy.

Now this Oriental said he didn't want to get involved in an arrest or go to court or anything—all he wanted was to get in his car and leave. The cops realized that the guy breaking into the car was a psycho, and the first one tried to move the guy on by prodding him with his nightstick. He wasn't holding the stick securely, and the guy grabbed it and started striking him across the neck with it. And across the face. And the cop went down.

The other cop drew his revolver but hesitated to fire because a crowd was beginning to gather around them. So it was like a standoff—the perp menacing them with a stick and the cops pointing their guns at him. It was about then that we showed up.

The first cop told us what'd happened, so we attempted to place the guy under arrest. We knocked him to the ground, but he continued fighting. I got hit across the shin, and when I tried to put handcuffs on him, he bit me on the hand.

By now, the crowd had gotten really big. People were coming out of Macy's, coming from all over, and what did they see? Four police officers and a black guy laying on the ground. That was the first thing they saw, all these Joe Liberal people. Especially this one well-dressed white guy who, all the time Brian was trying to control the crowd, kept on inciting people and yelling about "police brutality." And when Brian told him to shut up and get back on the sidewalk, he kept on yelling and demanding the names and badge numbers of the cops "who are beating up that man."

Apparently someone had called 911 and told them that there was a small riot going on outside Macy's because more police officers arrived and began to take control of the crowd. One of the cops from our Precinct showed up on a scooter, and as he was trying to get through the crowd, this other black guy—not the one that was trying to break into the car—said to him, "Now you're going to get yours!" And the guy tried to hit the cop with a ten-pound portable radio. The cop backed up, and then the guy stabbed him in the left hand with an umbrella.

Brian saw what was going on, and he grabbed the guy with the radio around the neck and pulled him down over the hood of a taxi that had been stopped by the crowd. And when it was all over, we all got in the radio car—me, Brian, the two Transit cops who'd been injured themselves, plus the two prisoners.

When we got to Bellevue, one of the prisoners only needed some stitches, but the other guy had a broken arm. A compound fracture, OK? Now the doctor had him on a table and he wanted him to turn over. But he told him not to lean on that arm. So the guy leaned on it. Like he was doing pushups. And he rolled right over on it. Just like it had never happened.

Case closed? Case *not* closed!

Because most of the crowd that gathered hadn't gotten there until long after the whole thing started, after the guy had taken the cop's nightstick. Because they started making all kinds of trouble for the two Transit cops. "Police brutality," all that shit.

Now fortunately, the cab driver was a witness—he'd even gotten blood on the front of his cab. And he came into the police station and gave a written report saying that the guy had hit the policeman with the nightstick and that the police officers had restrained themselves as best they could.

But for fourteen months, the Department hassled these two guys before they finally exonerated them.

Fourteen months!

So this black guy bites me on the hand, right? The guy on 35th Street and Sixth Avenue.

So you know what I wake up with the next morning? I wake up with this craving for watermelon. And ribs. And now, every time there's a full moon, I'm going to have to sing "Mammy."

This girl, a Hassidic Jew, was about nineteen, married, and eight months pregnant. She was supposed to meet her husband in the garment district, somewhere on 37th Street.

While she was waiting, this Puerto Rican guy came along, took her inside a building, choked her, raped her, and then while she was still alive, he threw her in a furnace. The furnace was on, and she burned to death.

But the body didn't burn completely, so he took it out and put it in the garbage. That's where they found it.

The next day, they caught him, the police from Midtown South. He got twenty years to life.

He'll probably be out in fifteen.

Take somebody like Son of Sam. Everybody gets in an outrage, they're ready to lynch the guy. But if he doesn't do it again, he'll be forgotten in a month.

The only people who will remember the grief he caused are the police and the families of the victims.

In 1967, there was a guy who placed an ad in the paper for a model. A girl named Susan Reynolds went there to Greenwich Village to apply for the job. When she walked in, he raped her and strangled her. And that was that.

The guy was captured. He went to jail, and after a while, some psychiatrist said, "It's out of his system now. He's cured, and he can go back in society."

So he came back out. And last year, he put another ad in the paper. And another girl showed up, he strangled her, and threw her out a window.

Okay, the guy's back in jail. But only until some other psychiatrist says, "Well, it's out of his system now." And then he'll be back out.

NO PRISONER TO LEAVE ARREST ROOM
FOR ANY REASON UNLESS HAND CUFFED
Lieut. CO. MTS

"Sector . . . any available car . . . ten thirty-three: Burger King . . . Four-six and Four-seven on Broadway . . . white man in plaid jacket armed with a shotgun . . ."

"Armed robbery in progress"—that's what 10-33 means. And you know it's happening in a place with a lot of people around. I mean, a Burger King isn't exactly Grant's Tomb, not with an address like Broadway between 46th and 47th. So we go blasting up there with our lights on and everything, turning on 46th Street—the wrong way. What's coming toward us from the other end of the block? Another car that's also responding to the call. And what do we see? A guy in a plaid jacket running toward us on the sidewalk. And the other police car is coming up behind him.

When the guy sees us, he doesn't know what to do. He slows down a little and then starts to take off his jacket. The way he's holding it—with one hand on the collar and the other down at the bottom somewhere—it looks like he's trying to hide something. We stop the car and get out. So do the two cops from the other car. We all have our pistols drawn—the guy is armed with a shotgun, right?—and we move toward him yelling, "Police! Halt!"

By now, the guy sees that he's surrounded. There's panic written all over this guy's face. He's got one hand down by his hip, and he's holding the other straight out in front of him with the rolled-up jacket pointed out into the street. . . .

Holy shit! This *is* a real one! And there are four cops out there thinking the same thing: If he swings his arms toward any of us, he's dead.

Then, all of a sudden, the guy, scared shit, drops the jacket and throws up his hands. Later, we find out what the story was: A young couple was in the Burger King and two guys come over and start insulting the girl. The guy she's with doesn't want to mess with the other two, so he calls 911, reports an armed robbery, and gives a description of the guy in the plaid jacket. Just to get rid of them.

So here was a 10-33 where, in fact, the suspect was *not* armed. But how is the cop out there supposed to know that? If I think a guy's going to hurt me, he's going to get shot. It's that simple. If a guy moves his arms in a way that I think he's got a weapon, I'll drop him. What would happen to me afterward? I just don't care. I'd go straight to the nearest bar and have a drink. And feel very good about it.

Perps 0, Cops 1.

There's front-cuffing and back-cuffing. Front-cuffing has nothing but disadvantages—the guy can hit you, bite you, choke you, pull your hair, do all kinds of stuff. A guy who's back-cuffed understands immediately that if he wants to play, he's going to lose. You might say he's in a more receptive mood. . . .

One day, a detective we know arrested this black guy—I don't know what the story was—but anyway, when his sheet came back, the guy was wanted by the North Carolina authorities. And they teletyped that they were going to send up two state troopers.

Now the black guy was a real bad-mouth turkey. Everything was "bullshit" and "motherfucker" and all of that. And he'd been running his mouth off ever since he was taken into custody.

So now the detective tells him that two cops are coming up from North Carolina to get him. The guy shits.

"They're going to kill me! They're going to put me out into a field there, and they're going to shoot me for escaping."

Now the guy is sitting in court with the detective when the two state troopers come walking in. And the *shorter* one is like six-four.

They have one of those waistbands with handcuffs on each side, so they manacle him, put chains on his feet, and march him outside. The turkey is like a little kid—head down, very meek, following the state troopers.

They get outside, and the detective asks if they need a ride to the airport. One of the state troopers says, "Nope, we rented a car."

And where is the car? Right up on the sidewalk in front of the courthouse.

The turkey walks to the back door, and the state trooper looks at him. "You ain't riding in the back of my car. I don't want to have to look at you all the way to the airport."

So he goes around to the back, opens the trunk, and says, "Get in, boy."

The turkey jumps right in, and the state trooper slams the trunk.

"Thank you, officer." From inside the trunk.

And off they went. Case closed.

The time was in the South—and it still may be—that when they got them alone, they did a job on them so that when it was time to handle them in public, there was no hassle. They'd just "sir" the shit out of them. You know, "yes sir, no sir, three bags full . . ."

Terror is the ultimate weapon.

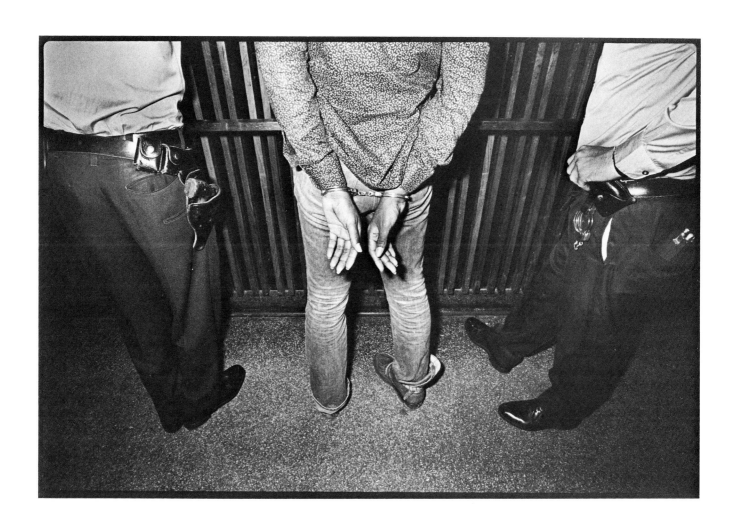

This was a call to a hotel on 43rd Street: *"aided case."* And when you've got an address like that, you need all the help you can get.

We get there and see this black guy lying in bed.

"Did you call for an ambulance? What's the matter?"

"Look—I don't need no ambulance," the guy says. "I don't want to go to the hospital, I'm OK. Like, just forget it."

All right, we cancel the ambulance, and we leave.

About an hour later, there's a second call. Same place, same guy. Just as we're getting there, the ambulance pulls up, so now there's four of us going to the room, including the driver and the attendant, who's a black guy.

"What's going on? You called before, the ambulance came out, we canceled it, and now you're calling again. What's the story?"

"Well, I got cut, see. . . ."

"Cut? It doesn't look like you're bleeding."

"But, like, I got cut . . . on my privates."

"You want to go to the hospital?"

"I don't know, man. This was just something between me and my old lady. I don't know what I want to do."

So now the attendant goes over to the bed.

"Cut the bullshit, man, and let me take a look."

Finally, the guy pulls down the sheet. His balls are literally hanging out of the sack—he must've been cut half a dozen times.

The attendant shows us what happened to the guy and tells him, "You better get your ass to the hospital, or you're going to be one dead nigger. I can tell you right now you're never going to have any kids. But if you let infection get in there, you're in a world of shit. . . ."

The guy's face goes pale. And it turned out that some young chick who used to live in the hotel came by his room, and while he was getting it on with her, his old lady comes and catches them in the rack. So she waits till he goes to sleep and takes a razor and slashes his balls. Six or seven times.

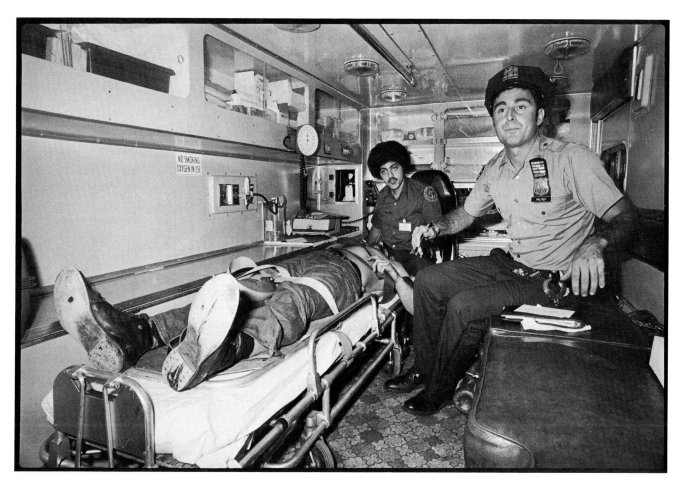

It's about five o'clock in the afternoon, and Jimmy and Mike are walking past one of the junk stores on 42nd Street, and they see this turkey yelling at the store owner. As they go over to check it out, the mutt goes out the door.

So they ask the counterman what was going on, and he tells them that the mutt was trying to buy a holster. They go out after him, and the mutt pulls a .38 and starts firing.

It's just like in the movies. People are running every which way. Mike and Jimmy start chasing him right down the middle of the street, and at the same time, calling on the radio for backup. Me and Brian are on 43rd Street between Eighth and Ninth Avenues.

The mutt gets to 42nd Street and Eighth Avenue and right there is a cop talking to a sergeant. The mutt sees them first, and he shoots the cop in the side of the chest and keeps running right down into the subway with Mike and Jimmy right behind him.

We get on the scene after driving a couple of blocks in reverse. The cop is down, bleeding from all over, and the humps from the Apple are all around him. A stray bullet has hit one of them.

We get to the injured cop, but we can't reach Mike and Jimmy because the radio doesn't work in the subway.

Now the perp gets away for a few seconds and jumps on a train and makes like he's just sitting there. Mike and Jimmy stop all the trains and begin searching. And who is the mutt sitting next to? An off-duty detective.

Just then, the mutt pulls the gun, but Jimmy and Mike can't get a shot in the crowded train. The off-duty detective grabs for the gun as Mike and Jimmy jump the mutt. They collar him after a fierce and violent struggle.

It turns out he's only sixteen years old. So nothing is going to happen to him.

The next day in the Port Authority Bus Terminal, a wino bum jumps a Port cop, knocks him down, rips the cop's gun from his holster, and shoots the cop in the face three times, killing him. Then the bum turns the gun on the people in the waiting room, shooting a few of them.

Finally another cop runs up and blows the bum's head off.

That's the Rotten Apple for you.

There's too much politics in New York. They don't give a shit about people here. It's all money.

To me, the only thing I think would help—not "help," I shouldn't use that word, let's say "change things"—is that some of these big-shot politicians themselves will have to get hurt.

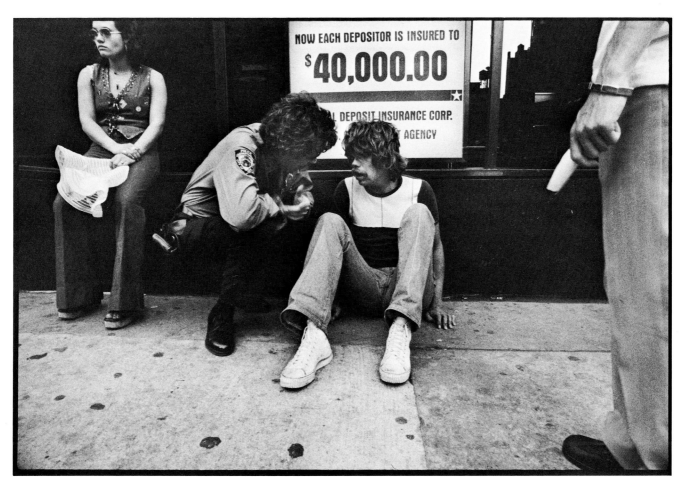

The State of New York has something like 22,000 jail cells for receiving convicted criminals. But because this is far too low a figure to take care of all those people who should, by anybody's standards, be in jail, judges and DAs either don't indict a large number of criminals or else they reduce the charges against them, usually down to "misdemeanor."

In one year alone, the overcrowding of jails in this state resulted in what is called "early release" for a little over 18,000 convicts—simply because the jails couldn't handle them.

And where are they now? More than 14,000 of them live in New York City.

And what were they convicted of? Armed robbery, kidnapping, arson, murder, rape . . .

"There is no morale on the New York police force. The job is burned out. . . ."

"I don't know if that's true. There are a lot of good cops out there doing an almost impossible job under extremely difficult circumstances. And they're enjoying it. Maybe we're the ones that are burned out. Maybe we've seen too much, too many crazy things. . . ."

"But the post you and Timmy had, for instance . . ."

"Look, some young kid's going to come along, and he'll get that post. And he'll be full of piss and vinegar. And he'll do all the things he has to do to make that post what it should be. *His post.*"

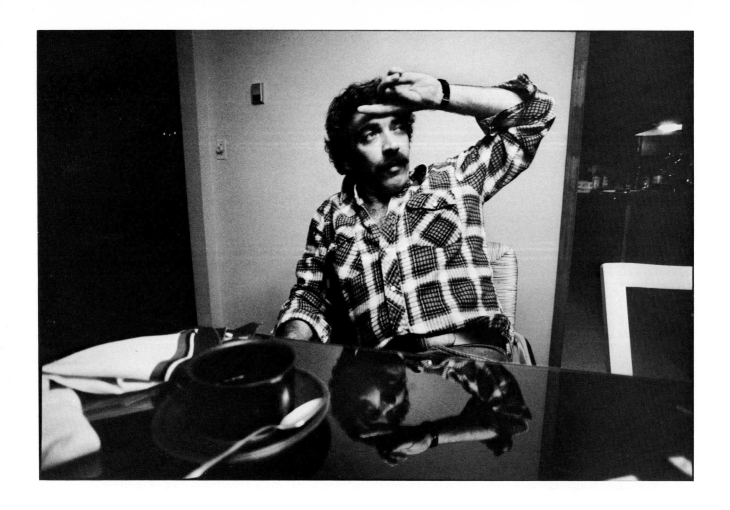

On July 13, 1980, a car driven by a young woman ran into the motorcycle ridden by Gene Gentile. Gene, who was on his way to buy a present for his son's birthday, suffered a severely crushed foot that has required more than forty operations and is the source of constant pain.

In 1981, "Kid Blast" was retired from the force by a Medical Review Board, and he now spends a lot of time thinking about Sector Adam in Midtown South.

Since Gene's accident and retirement, Brian McMenamin has had other partners—young cops at the beginning of their careers, old cops at the end of theirs. "Professor Snake" finally put in a demand to work alone on a foot post. He could not find a partner as good as Gene.

Brian is planning to leave the New York Police Department.

our thanks to

Frank McLoughlin
Deputy Commissioner
of the New York City Police Department
for the authorization
that allowed us to produce this book

Dick Seaver
our publisher, for his confidence,
and for his understanding
of what this book set out to do

Christian Guillon
for his help with the layout

Pictorial Service
Paris